AF270570

"David Bell has brought to life a fascinating chapter in the larger-than-life image of Bernard of Clairvaux created by the misattribution of many works to this revered Cistercian author. *The Very Devout Meditations,* with a medieval transmission that far exceeded any of Bernard's authentic works and a readership that continued into the twentieth century, offers a compelling path toward claiming a place in the heavenly kingdom, a process fueled by the terrors of hell and requiring knowledge of the true nature of the self. Bell's erudite introduction and careful identification of sources complement the vivid translation, making the volume a great introduction to the rich field of Cistercian spirituality beyond the already well-known giants like Bernard."

> —Anne L. Clark, Professor Emerita of Religion, University of Vermont

"Who knew that the most popular work by Bernard of Clairvaux in the medieval period was not by Bernard at all? David Bell presents this influential anonymous work to modern English audiences with a thorough introduction and essential notes. As usual, David Bell is as entertaining as he is effortlessly erudite. This work will appeal to everyone who is interested in the way Bernard was perceived in the centuries following his death and, in general, the way in which reputation and authorship were transmitted and transformed in medieval Europe."

> —Fr. Lawrence Morey, Abbey of Gethsemani

CISTERCIAN STUDIES SERIES: NUMBER TWO HUNDRED NINETY-EIGHT

The Very Devout Meditations attributed to Bernard of Clairvaux

A Translation with Introduction and Notes
of the *Meditationes piisimae
de cognitione humanae conditionis*
by David N. Bell

Cistercian Publications
www.cistercianpublications.org

LITURGICAL PRESS
Collegeville, Minnesota
www.litpress.org

A Cistercian Publications title published by Liturgical Press

Cistercian Publications
Editorial Offices
161 Grosvenor Street
Athens, Ohio 45701
www.cistercianpublications.org

© 2023 by David N. Bell

Published by Liturgical Press, Collegeville, Minnesota. All rights reserved. No part of this book may be used or reproduced in any manner whatsoever, except brief quotations in reviews, without written permission of Liturgical Press, Saint John's Abbey, PO Box 7500, Collegeville, MN 56321-7500. Printed in the United States of America.

1   2   3   4   5   6   7   8   9

Library of Congress Cataloging-in-Publication Data

Names: Bernard, of Clairvaux, Saint, 1090 or 1091-1153 author. | Bell, David
    N., 1943– translator.
Title: The very devout meditations attributed to Bernard of Clairvaux : a
    translation, with introduction and notes, of the Meditationes piisimae de
    cognitione humanae conditionis / by David N. Bell.
Other titles: Meditationes piisimae de cognitione humanae conditionis. English
Description: Collegeville, Minnesota : Cistercian Publications, [2023] | Series:
    Cistercian studies series ; no. two hundred ninety-eight | Translation of:
    Meditationes piisimae de cognitione humanae conditionis. | Includes
    bibliographical references and index. | Summary: "This volume, the first
    complete translation in more than three-hundred years, presents one of
    the most important texts in the history of medieval Latin spirituality.
    Written between 1170 and 1190 by an unidentified Cistercian monk-priest,
    Meditationes piisimae, "Very Devout Meditations," became one of the
    most popular and widely distributed pieces of spiritual literature in the
    whole of the Middle Ages. The work survives in at least 670 manuscripts
    with the complete English translation of the treatise published in 1701"—
    Provided by publisher.
Identifiers: LCCN 2023018123 (print) | LCCN 2023018124 (ebook) | ISBN
    9780879071578 (trade paperback) | ISBN 9780879071585 (epub) | ISBN
    9780879072162 (pdf)
Subjects: LCSH: Spiritual life—Catholic Church. | Meditations.
Classification: LCC BX2179.B472 M4413 2023 (print) | LCC BX2179.B472
    (ebook) | DDC 271/.1202—dc23/eng/20230627
LC record available at https://lccn.loc.gov/2023018123
LC ebook record available at https://lccn.loc.gov/2023018124

To the memory of
Sister Jane Patricia Freeland
(1910–2004)

Contents

List of Abbreviations   ix

Part One: Introduction

Chapter One: Bernard and Pseudo-Bernard   3

Chapter Two: The *Meditationes piisimae*   19

Chapter Three: The Teaching of the *Meditationes*: Theory   37

Chapter Four: The Teaching of the *Meditationes*: Practice   55

Chapter Five: The English Translations   71

Part Two: The Translation

*Most Devout Meditations
On the Knowledge of the Human Condition*

Chapter One: On Human Dignity   89

Chapter Two: On Human Misery, the Horror of Death,
and the Severity of the Supreme Judge   95

Chapter Three: Of the Dignity of the Soul and the Baseness
of the Body   101

Chapter Four: Of the Reward of the Heavenly Homeland   109

Chapter Five: On the Daily Examination of Oneself   116

Chapter Six: On the Need to Be Attentive at the Time
of Prayer   119

Chapter Seven: On Guarding the Heart and Zeal in Prayer   126

Chapter Eight: On the Hatred of Carelessness or Negligence
in Prayer   128

Chapter Nine: On the Unstable Nature of the Human
Heart   130

Chapter Ten: On the Dislike of Being Corrected,
and of Being Accused of One's Failures and Faults   135

Chapter Eleven: On Conscience, Which Accompanies Us
Everywhere and Continually Goads Us   141

Chapter Twelve: Of the Three Enemies of Humankind:
The Flesh, the World, and the Devil   142

Chapter Thirteen: On the Attacks of These Three
Aforesaid Enemies   146

Chapter Fourteen: On the Desire for Our Heavenly Homeland
and on Its Supreme Happiness   148

Chapter Fifteen: On the Nature and Feelings of the Old Self,
and Its Mortification and Transformation through Christ   150

Index of Classical, Patristic, and Medieval Sources   155

Index of Names and Subjects in Part One   159

List of Abbreviations

Bell, "Bibliography"	"A Bibliography of English Translations of Works by and Attributed to St Bernard of Clairvaux: 1496–1970." *Cîteaux—Commentarii cistercienses* 48 (1997): 83–129.
BHL	*Bibliotheca hagiographica latina antiquae et mediae aetatis*. Brussels, 1898–1901; repr. 1949, 1992.
Bultot, "Les 'Meditationes'"	Robert Bultot. "Les 'Meditationes' Pseudo-Bernardines sur la connaissance de la condition humaine. Problèmes d'histoire littéraire." *Sacris Erudiri* 15 (1964): 256–92. (In the list of contents of this volume of *Sacris Erudiri*, the article is ascribed to Roger Baron and Robert Bultot, but the title page of the article mentions only Bultot.)
CCCM	Corpus Christianorum Continuatio Mediaevalis. Turnhout: Brepols.
CF	Cistercian Fathers Series. Cistercian Publications.
CPL	Eligius Dekkers and Aemilius Gaar, Clavis Patrum Latinorum. 3rd ed. Turnhout: Brepols, 1995.
CS	Cistercian Studies Series. Cistercian Publications.

Giraud,
Spiritualité   Cédric Giraud. *Spiritualité et histoire des textes entre Moyen Âge et époque moderne: Genèse et fortune d'un corpus pseudépigraphe de méditations*. Série Moyen Âge et Temps Modernes 52. Paris: Institut d'Études Augustiniennes, 2016.

LLT   Library of Latin Texts, Series A and Series B. Turnhout: Brepols.

PHI   Packard Humanities Institute Classical Latin Texts

PL   Patrologia Cursus Completus, Series Latina

RSB   Regula sancti Benedicti

SBOp   Sancti Bernardi Opera. Ed. Jean Leclercq, C. Hugh Talbot, and Henri M. Rochais. Rome: Editiones Cistercienses, 1957–1977.

SCO   Sources chrétiennes Online. Turnhout: Brepols.

Walther, Initia   Hans Walther. *Initia carminum ac versuum medii aevi posterioris latinorum*. Göttingen, 1959.

PART ONE

Introduction

CHAPTER ONE

Bernard and Pseudo-Bernard

The first thing we all need to do is to change our perspective. It is too easy to put the authentic Bernard on a pedestal, and treat the multitudinous *ps.*-Bernards as second-class citizens, or perhaps second-class *spirituels*, not worth a second glance and certainly not worth a critical edition. Nothing could be more inappropriate. As we shall see, there were times and places where *ps.*-Bernard was unquestionably more popular than Bernard himself, and the various treatises that circulated under his name were widely read and widely distributed. In 2016, Cédric Giraud published an exhaustive study of these pseudonymous works,[1] a study of superlative and essential scholarship, but although he adds much to our understanding of these neglected works, there is still more to be said on the subject of the *Meditationes piisimae*.

In 2016, Cistercian Publications published English translations of three of these *ps.*-Bernardine works—the *Formula honestae vitae*, the *Instructio sacerdotalis*, and the *Tractatus de statu virtutum humilitatis, obedientiae, timoris, et charitatis*—with an excellent introduction by Dom Elias Dietz of the Abbey of

---

1. Cédric Giraud, *Spiritualité et histoire des textes entre Moyen Âge et époque moderne: Genèse et fortune d'un corpus pseudépigraphe de méditations*, Série Moyen Âge et Temps Modernes 52 (Paris: Institut d'Études Augustiniennes, 2016). Cited as in the List of Abbreviations as Giraud, *Spiritualité*.

Gethsemani.[2] A few years earlier, in 2010, Mark DelCogliano had published translations of two other such works, the *Speculum monachorum* of Arnulf of Bohéries, and the *Octo puncta perfectionis assequendae*, which the author suggests, tentatively, may also have been composed by Arnulf.[3] These translations are welcome, and they happily represent a new interest in this important literature. In earlier centuries, English translation of *ps.*-Bernardine works were far from uncommon, and in an article I published in 1970,[4] I pointed out there that the earliest English translations of "Bernard" were not of Bernard himself, but of *ps.*-Bernard, and that that tradition was hardly to change for more than three hundred years.[5] The very first English translation of any work by or attributed to Bernard to be published in England was the 1496 translation of the *ps.*-Bernardine *Meditationes piisimae*.[6]

I admit that I do not care for Professor DelCogliano's distinction of a Cistercian "Golden Age" followed by a "Silver Age"—this is too easily misunderstood—but he is certainly correct when he states that the shift from "Gold" to "Silver"

> is not a decline or a decay or a corruption; rather, it is a slow-
> ing down, a taking stock, a reflection upon a great achieve-

2. *Three Pseudo-Bernardine Works*, trans./annot. Catena Scholarum, intro. Dom Elias Dietz, CS 273 (Collegeville, MN: Cistercian Publications, 2018). The *Formula honestae vitae* had previously been translated in 1613, 1620, and 1631: see Bell, "Bibliography," 95, 97.

3. Mark DelCogliano, "Cistercian Monasticism in the Silver Age: Two Texts on Practical Advice," *Cistercian Studies Quarterly* 45 (2010): 421–52. An earlier translation of the *Octo puncta* dates from 1631: see Bell, "Bibliography," 97.

4. David N. Bell, " 'In Their Mother Tongue': A Brief History of the English Translation of Works by and Attributed to Saint Bernard of Clairvaux: 1496–1970," in *The Joy of Learning and the Love of God: Studies in Honor of Jean Leclercq*, ed. E. Rozanne Elder, CS 160 (Kalamazoo, MI/Spencer, MA: Cistercian Publications, 1995), 291–308.

5. Bell, " 'In Their Mother Tongue,' " 291. I shall return to this article in chap. 5.

6. Bell, "Bibliography," 90–91. We shall examine this translation in some detail in chap. 5.

ment, a thoughtful and loving reception of an enormous legacy, by people intent on being worthy heirs to the giants who preceded them. . . . Earlier Cistercians had expressed the theory, or perhaps the theology, of Cistercian spirituality, and subsequent Cistercians felt the need to articulate its practice. The Cistercian silver age was perhaps a time of reduced horizons, but it was no less ardent in its contemplative desire for God.[7]

But we must be careful with our terminology here. In his *Scala claustralium*, Guigo II of la Chartreuse distinguishes clearly between contemplation and meditation. "Meditation [*meditatio*]," he says,

> is the studious action of the mind, seeking out the understanding of a hidden truth under the direction of one's own reason. Contemplation [*contemplatio*] is when the mind is in some way lifted up to God and suspended above itself, tasting the joys of everlasting sweetness.[8]

In other words, for Guigo, meditation is active and discursive and makes use of the intellect and the imagination; contemplation is passive and experiential and is entirely dependent on God. The *ps.*-Bernardine works, and especially the *Meditationes piisimae* that are our concern here, tend not to make this distinction. There are, of course, numerous passages in Bernard's authentic works in which he speaks of contemplation in precisely the way that Guigo explains it, but such passages are hardly ever to be found in the anonymous *ps.*-Bernardine literature. There is nothing mystical about the *Meditationes*, if by mystical we mean a direct unmediated experience of God that may be achieved, if rarely and briefly, in this life—the sort of experience described by Bernard in his *De*

---

7. DelCogliano, "Cistercian Monasticism," 423–24.

8. Guigues II le Chartreux, *Lettre sur la vie contemplative; Douze méditations*, ed. Edmund Colledge and James Walsh; trans. Un Chartreux, SCh 163 (Paris: Cerf, 1970), 84.

diligendo Deo or by Richard of Saint-Victor in his *Benjamin minor* and *Benjamin major*. But these mystical heights, these Himalayas of the soul, were never for the average monk or nun, and, as André Vauchez has said, we need "to bring the history of spirituality down from the summits where it has too often been pleased to dwell,"[9] and cease confining it to the experiences of what he calls a "limited élite."[10] Putting it another way, the *Meditationes* are spiritual, but not mystical, and all the more profitable for that.

The verb, the adjective, and the noun—*contemplo, contemplativus,* and *contemplatio*—are all to be found in the *Meditationes,*[11] but apart from the contemplation of God in Paradise, the Beatific Vision itself, when this life is over, "to contemplate" is best translated as to reflect on, muse on, think about, ruminate, or ponder. It is essentially the equivalent of Saint Bernard's "consideration" (*consideratio*).

How many of these *ps.*-Bernardine works are there? In 1891, Leopold Janauschek listed no fewer than 177 titles,[12] though a good many of these are different titles for the same work. Of these, 120 are prose and 57 verse. A more practical list was provided in 1932 by Ferdinand Cavallera in the first volume of the *Dictionnaire de spiritualité.*[13] Cavallera divides his list into "Extracts or reworkings of authentic works" (five entries), "Works restored to their true authors" (twenty-nine entries), "Apocryphal works by unknown authors" (thirty-eight entries), and a final section on the *ps.*-Bernardine poems, including the rather lovely *Jubilus rhythmicus de nomine Jesu* (PL 184:317–20). Additions and corrections

9. André Vauchez, trans. Colette Friedlander, *The Spirituality of the Medieval West: The Eighth to the Twelfth Century,* CS 145 (Kalamazoo, MI: Cistercian Publications, 1993), 10.

10. Vauchez, *Spirituality of the Medieval West,* 168.

11. The noun three times, the verb and adjective once each.

12. See Leopold Janauschek, *Bibliographia Bernardina* (Vienna: A. Hölder, 1891; repr. Hildesheim: G. Olms, 1959), iv–xiv.

13. Ferdinand Cavallera, "Bernard (Apocryphes attribués à saint)," in *Dictionnaire de spiritualité* (Paris: Beauchesne, 1932), 1:1499–1502.

to this material have been made, and continue to be made, by later research. The *Meditationes* are number 15 in column 1500, and the author states that "they deserve to be studied more closely." They have been.

A different approach is to be found in Dom Elias Dietz's survey, "Toward a Canon of Pseudo-Bernard Works," that appeared in 2016.[14] Here Dom Elias takes just eleven texts that he considers "worthwhile" and divides them into four categories. The first he calls the *De conscientia* treatises: "highly introspective in character, these texts are meant to encourage the moral reform of the person from within." Here he includes the *Meditationes*, as well as the *De interiori domo* and the anonymous *De conscientia* (not that of Peter of Celle). The second group are "Short works of practical advice or so-called mirrors." Here we find two works translated in the volume in which Dom Elias's survey appears—the *Formula honestae vitae* and the *Tractatus de statu virtutum humilitatis, obedientiae, timoris, et charitati*—and the two treatises translated by Mark DelCogliano, the *Speculum monachorum* and the *Octo puncta perfectionis assequendae*. The fifth is the *Doctrina sancti Bernardi* (PL 184:1177–82). These are followed by two "Meditations on the Passion"—*Lamentatio in Passionem Christi* (PL 184:769–72) and *Rhythmus ad singular membra Christi patientis* (PL 184:1319–24)—and one final "Devotional text," the *Jubilus Rhythmicus de Nomine Jesu* (PL 184:317–20).

This is obviously a personal selection, and not everyone will agree with it. Personally, if I find Janauschek's list too long, I find Dom Elias's list too short. There are other works that I myself would certainly consider worthwhile that might be added to it, but that is something best discussed over a glass or two of good wine. One thing remains clear: with the work of Cédric Giraud we have certainly made a good beginning in the study of these anonymous *ps.*-Bernardine texts, but it is equally clear that there is still a long way to go.

14. See *Three Pseudo-Bernardine Works*, 7–10.

There can be no doubt that many of these works, before they were restored to their true authors, owed their popularity to the name of Bernard. At the risk of stating the obvious, his name was known throughout Europe, and his genuine writings enjoyed wide circulation. He was deeply involved in politics, both secular and ecclesiastical, he had the ear of popes and princes, and he was an ardent heresy hunter, though he did not always understand the subtleties of the heresies he was hunting. He had his finger in a multitude of pies—David Crouch refers to him as "that European busybody"[15]—and whether you liked him or not, you certainly knew his name. It is quite possible, for example, that if the *De contemplando Deo* of William of Saint-Thierry had not circulated under the name of Bernard, it might hardly have been noticed.

A glance at Cavallera's list reveals many famous names, or, more precisely, names that are famous now but were, I suspect, less celebrated at the time the manuscripts were circulated. There was William of Saint-Thierry, for example, and Aelred of Rievaulx, Guigo II of la Chartreuse, Hugh and Richard of Saint-Victor, and a number of others. That they all benefited from having their works circulating under the name of the European busybody cannot be doubted. But there are still many works listed whose true authors remain unknown. What is the value of these works?

Dom Elias refers to a number of areas in which their historical importance was considerable. He points out that anonymity gave the writers "greater freedom of expression in presenting traditional material in an experiential, personal key," and that they were "particularly conducive to meditative reading."[16] Giraud discusses this last point at great length and shows how the Western concept of the nature and practice of meditation was molded by these texts.[17] The same is true of the later Western concept of *conscientia* or

---

15. David Crouch, *The Reign of King Stephen: 1135–1154* (New York: Longman, 2000), 309.

16. *Three Pseudo-Bernardine Works*, 5.

17. Giraud, *Spiritualité, passim,* but especially 37–117.

conscience. In these texts, conscience is not only a consciousness
of one's own sinfulness, of the loss of likeness to the image of
God, though that is certainly there, but also a call to repentance
and self-responsibility, and to that change in one's way of life that
is an essential part of the spiritual path. "I cannot hide my sins,"
says the author of the *Meditationes*,

> for wherever I go my conscience is with me, carrying with
> it whatever I have put there, whether good or evil. It keeps
> safe everything that has been entrusted to it while I am alive,
> and it will give it back to me when I am dead. If I do evil,
> it is there; and if I seem to have done well, and have been
> praised for it, it is there. It is there while I am alive; it fol-
> lows me in death. (§32)

Conscience, in fact, overlaps with self-knowledge, for as Peter
of Celle defined it in his important treatise *De conscientia*, written
in about 1180 and addressed to Alcher of Clairvaux,[18] conscience
is "knowledge of itself, either choosing good or avoiding evil."[19]
In other words, our conscience may both cause us grief and act
as a goad. On the one hand, because of my guilty conscience,
says the author of the *Meditationes*, "I shall stand, trembling and
anxious, before the Lord in Judgment, recalling all the wicked
deeds I have ever committed" (§4). On the other, by holding God
in our memory and carrying him in our conscience (§2), we are
goaded to turn from the things of this world to the things that
pertain to God, and to begin (by God's grace) the restoration of
the lost likeness. How? It is simple. As Peter of Celle said, by
choosing good and avoiding evil. On the other hand, of course,
if I may quote the incomparable R. Austin Freeman, "it seems to

---

18. PL 202:1083D–97A. There is a good English translation by Hugh Feiss
in *Peter of Celle: Selected Works*, trans. Hugh Feiss, CS 100 (Kalamazoo, MI:
Cistercian Publications, 1987), 143–88.

19. *Conscientia est sui ipsius scientia vel de bono sumens, vel de malo dis-
sidens* (PL 202:1098A).

be the fact that some fortunate persons have no conscience at all; a negative gift that raises them above the mental vicissitudes of the common herd of humanity."[20]

Dom Elias also points out how important some of these texts were for the instruction of novices, and the *Octo puncta perfectionis assequendae,* "Eight Points for Attaining Perfection," is a good example, not least because of its parallels with the *Meditationes* (PL 184:1181–90).[21] The first point is the need for frequent confession, and confession that is pure and complete, *purus* and *integer.* It must also be done with great sorrow, and the intention not to repeat the offences. The author of the *Meditationes* says just the same thing: confession must be frequent, pure, and true. The second point is not to be disheartened by adversity or temptation, for overcoming obstacles is a necessary part of life in general, and the religious life in particular. It is the devil's business to tempt us, says the author of the *Meditationes,* and there is nothing that so strengthens the soul against temptations as the contemplation of heavenly things (§21). The third point is the need to maintain one's monastic solitude, to be alone with Christ, one's spouse: "Don't mingle with people, either inside or outside the [monastery], so long as you can do this in a good way" (PL 184:1181D). Avoid worldly gossip and fatuous worldly conversations, for they will only distract and disquiet the mind.

The fourth point is critical: "At all times you should cultivate purity of heart, so that by continually closing off the bodily senses, you may return to yourself" (PL 184:1181D). How is this to be done? By keeping control of one's thoughts and desires, and directing our heart and mind unswervingly to God and the contemplation of divine things. The author of the *Octo puncta* elaborates

20. R. Austin Freeman, *The Famous Cases of Dr. Thorndyke* (London: Hodder & Stoughton, 1929), 3.

21. English translation by DelCogliano in "Cistercian Monasticism in the Silver Age," 441–51. In the paragraphs that follow, however, all translations are my own.

on this at some length, and what he says is directly paralleled in the *Meditationes*: "Restore yourself to yourself, and if not always or often, at least from time to time. Control your longings, direct your actions, amend your ways. Let nothing disorderly remain in you" (§14). The author of the *Meditationes* also has much to say on this matter, pointing out the fickle nature of the human heart, how it runs hither and thither at a whim, and part of the title of the seventh chapter is "On guarding the heart."

The fifth point is simpler. A monk should not be saddened, happy, or concerned about his friends or relatives. Pray for them and entrust them to God, and concentrate on the *interiora*, the inward things, where God is to be found.

In the sixth point, the teaching of the *Octo puncta* is once again that of the *Meditationes*. The author demands fervent prayer and holy meditation, though as we saw above, there is no mention of meditation in the *Meditationes*. There is, however, a great deal on prayer. Chapter six deals with the need to be wholly attentive to one's prayers, chapter seven emphasizes the need for zeal in prayer, and chapter eight points out the dangers of carelessness or negligence when praying. And when the author of the *Octo puncta* goes on to discuss the importance of fraternal correction and its immense value for spiritual progress—we are still with the sixth point—we may compare the tenth chapter of the *Meditationes*, with its discussion of the Chapter of Faults *in capitulo*, in the Chapter Room, which the *Octo puncta* does not mention.

The seventh and eighth points are straightforward and are taken directly from the Rule of Saint Benedict. First of all, be silent and don't talk too much (see RSB 6.2-4; 7.56). And if you have to speak, speak "softly and slowly, in a low voice, with a calm expression, and in a courteous manner" (PL 184:1185A). And second, *nunquam sis otiosus*, "you should never be idle," but the author does not tell us, as we might expect him to tell us, following the Rule of Saint Benedict, that "idleness is the enemy of the soul [*inimica animae*]." He tells us instead that idleness is "the death of the soul [*mors animae*]," an expression that occurs nowhere else in any of the standard databases (PL 184:1186A). This leads him to provide a brief outline of the monastic day and its duties, with spiritual things (such as reading, praying, or meditating) at spiritual times, and corporeal things (primarily manual labor) at corporeal times. This we do not find in the *Meditationes*. Subtle changes such as *mors* for *inimica* are not uncommon in the pseudonymous literature and do not make the hunt for sources any easier.

Thus, by following these eight points, the novice, or anybody else for that matter, will progress from virtue to virtue (Ps 83:8), gradually moving forwards but always being conscious of how far there is to go. "But be wary of the wiles of the devil, lest he lure you away from them!" (PL 184:1186B).

This is good, clear, practical, straightforward, down-to-earth spiritual teaching. There are no flights into mystical raptures here, no mystical marriages that the great Teresa of Àvila likened to rain falling in a river, when there is nothing there but water and it is no longer possible to separate the water of the river from that which fell from the heavens,[22] no Bernardine fourth degree of love wherein we love ourselves only for God's sake. These *ps.-*Bernardine works are not for the Olympic athletes of the spiritual path, but for the ordinary men and women, good, average monks and nuns, who were and are struggling to achieve, as best they can, that overcoming of self-love and self-will that lies at the heart of the spiritual path.

If some of the anonymous works seem addressed to novices and monks, others are directed more to priests. Such is the *Instructio sacerdotalis* (PL 184:771–92), which is an attempt to explain the mystery of the Mass, using Scripture, established authorities such as the fathers of the church, and "appropriate examples." The author certainly refers to himself as *frater Bernardus,* but he is certainly not Bernard of Clairvaux. A far more likely candidate is the Cluniac Bernard of Morlaix.[23] The writer divides the work

---

22. Teresa of Àvila, *The Interior Castle*, VII.2, 4.
23. See *Three Pseudo-Bernardine Works*, 13–14.

into three parts based on the three ways in which Christ gives himself to us. First, he gives himself to us on the cross for our redemption. Second, he gives himself to us in the Eucharist. And third, he gives himself to us as the gift of eternal life when our life on earth is over.

The author begins, logically enough, with the Fall of humankind in the Garden of Eden and the loss of our likeness to God. He spends some time, in fact, on what it means to be created *ad imaginem Dei*, and then goes on to show how we have fallen "from life to death, from incorruption to corruption, from freedom to servitude, from glory to punishment, from innocence to guilt, from the homeland into exile, from joy to sorrow, from blessedness to misery, from rest to toil."[24] We continued to stray from the time of the Fall to the time of Abraham, and then, from the time of Abraham to the time of the Redeemer, was the time of recalling (*revocatio*), when faith in the Trinity began to blossom and flourish. This was followed by the time of reconciliation, from the birth of Christ to his saving death on the cross, and then by the time of pilgrimage, which began with the coming of the Holy Spirit and will last until the end of the world. There then follows a long excursus in which "the whole work of human redemption is briefly explained."[25]

We now come to the heart of the *Instructio*, the doctrine of the Eucharist. He who gave himself to us once and for all as the *redemptionis pretium*, the price of redemption, now gives himself to us daily in the Eucharist. This is the subject of the whole of chapter seven, in which the writer dwells on *claritas*, the clarity or brilliance of the body of Christ in the radiance of the Godhead, in the glory of the incarnation, and in the mystery of the Eucharist. And what is his conclusion?

> The brilliance of the incarnate Word remains in his gloried humanity. It persists in him who has been set at the right hand of the Father. It will not diminish with time, it will not decrease

---

24. *Instructio*, I.2; PL 184:774D.
25. *Instructio*, VI.7–14; PL 184:776C–80C.

with time, nothing darkens it. It is just as glorious on the altar as it is in the heights of heaven, and it shines forth no less in the hands of the priest than in the bosom of God the Father.[26]

This leads naturally to the eighth chapter, which deals with the dignity of the priest and the high demands made of him. For not only is it the true Son of God who comes to the priest at the altar and whom the priest sacrifices and consumes; it is the whole Trinity! The Son comes, but not without the Father. The Son comes, but not without the Holy Spirit. And more than that, the whole heavenly host is also present. And since only a priest can transubstantiate—the writer uses the verb *transubstantiare*[27]—the dignity of a priest is greater than that of the angels! How much more, then, should a priest live a life worthy of this dignity, and how much should he prepare himself to celebrate the sacred mysteries. Such are the subjects of chapters nine to eleven.

Chapter twelve deals with the three ways in which a priest and his congregation might receive the Body and Blood of Christ: the first is sacramental and spiritual, the second spiritual, and the third only sacramental. The first way refers to the priest, who regularly received both the consecrated bread and wine. The second refers to the ordinary faithful, who did not normally receive communion, and if they did, it was but rarely.[28] But "even if they do not touch the sacrament with their mouth, they still obtain for themselves the power of the sacrament, that is, the remission of sins and the infusion of spiritual grace, through faith and union with the Church."[29] The third way, the sacramental alone, is damnable and hateful to God, for this applies to people who receive the sacrament unworthily or with lack of faith, and the author quotes 1 Corinthians 11:29 to prove his case: "Whoever eats and drinks unworthily, eats and drinks judgment to himself."

26. *Instructio*, VII.20; PL 184:784AB.
27. See *Three Pseudo-Bernardine Works*, 62, n. 77.
28. See *Three Pseudo-Bernardine Works*, 70, n. 93.
29. *Instructio*, XII.30; PL 184:789AB.

So what happens if we do take the sacrament unworthily? We go to hell, and in chapter fourteen we have a splendidly grisly description of the punishments that await those who have the misfortune to go there. What do we have? We have the nine punishments of hammer, stench, worms, fire, cold, demons, darkness, shame, and chains of fire. The writer then elaborates on all of these, but there is no corresponding description of the joys of Paradise such as we find in the *Meditationes*. It may be that this has been lost, for the treatise ends abruptly with demons laughing at the dreadful plight of the damned.

We must remember, of course, that for men and women in the twelfth century, death was an ever-present reality, and hell was not the Great Perhaps that François Rabelais was going to seek, but a grim and inevitable reality. For the peasantry in the twelfth century, those who worked the land, if they survived infancy (and infant mortality was appallingly high), they would have been lucky to reach their late thirties. Within the cloister, the life span was longer, not least because of better food, better drink, better care, and better hygiene. Taking a sample of a couple of dozen twelfth-century monks whose birth and death dates are fairly well established, most of them died between the ages of about 63 and 73. Even Aelred of Rievaulx, whose later years were plagued by sickness, survived to about 57. But however old they were, as death approached, they all had a very real fear of hell.

Descriptions of hell and purgatory are abundant,[30] and there is nothing unusual in the descriptions in the *Instructio*. There is no doubt that the threat of hell was a very useful tool in the hands

---

30. See Eileen Gardiner, *Medieval Visions of Heaven and Hell: A Sourcebook*, Garland Medieval Bibliographies (New York and London: Garland Publishing, 1993). There is an enormous literature on hell and purgatory in the Middle Ages, but for our present purposes I shall refer to just two studies: Alan E. Bernstein, "Heaven, Hell and Purgatory: 1100–1500," in *The Cambridge History of Christianity,* vol. 4, *Christianity in Western Europe, c. 1100–c. 1500,* ed. Miri Rubin (Cambridge: Cambridge University Press, 2009), 200–16; and Bart D. Ehrman, *Heaven and Hell: A History of the Afterlife* (New York: Simon and Schuster, 2020).

of the Church—it served to keep people in order—and since the only way to avoid punishment after death was to have one's sins absolved, and since absolution was normally given by a priest, we can understand the emphasis on complete and frequent confession that we find in the *ps.*-Bernardine and many other works. We will say much more about the importance of confession in chapter three.

These two brief works we have discussed, the *Octo puncta* and the *Instructio*, are good examples of this *ps.*-Bernadine literature, and the *Meditationes*, of course, are similar to the first of the two. It is not written for priests, though the author was himself a priest, and I think we may call it spiritual, psychological, pastoral, and personal. It is certainly not mystical, as we have defined the term above. That these *ps.*-Bernardine works were widely read is not in doubt, but as Dom Elias has said, "the fact that the Pseudo-Bernardine works were popular and accessible in the Middle Ages is no guarantee that they will appeal to a modern audience."[31] Indeed not. Although we live in an age of global warming, political chicanery, pandemics, and all the other problems the flesh is heir to, our life expectancy is much longer than that of our medieval ancestors, infant mortality far less, and an infinite number of the diseases to which men and women in the Middle Ages would inevitably have succumbed are now easily cured. The repellent descriptions of the human body and its functions, the depictions of death, and so on, are not much to our modern taste, but we must remember that they were always meant to be repellent. And what we read in the *Meditationes*, and in even more lurid detail in the *De miseria conditionis humanae* of Pope Innocent III, written when he was still Lotario dei Segni,[32] may well turn our delicate modern stomachs.

31. *Three Pseudo-Bernardine Works*, 10.

32. *Lotario dei Segni (Pope Innocent III). De Miseria Condicionis Humanae*, ed./trans. Robert E. Lewis, The Chaucer Library (Athens, GA: University of Georgia Press, 1978).

As to the torments of the damned, since the seventeenth century we have seen what Daniel Walker described as "the decline of hell,"[33] and although there are still plenty of people who have a literal belief in the worms and fire and gnashing of teeth that we find in the New Testament, there are certainly plenty who do not. When Sister Penelope Lawson published an edited translation of the *Instructio* in 1954, she omitted almost all of the descriptions of the torments of hell on the grounds that such crude medieval realism "does not commend itself to modern minds."[34] It probably does not, but it is not the translator's business to modernize the Middle Ages. What follows in the second part of this little book is a complete and unexpurgated English translation of the *Meditationes*, the first in more than three hundred years, and nothing has been omitted at all. Let us therefore take an initial glance at this astonishingly popular work.

33. Daniel P. Walker, *The Decline of Hell: Seventeenth-Century Discussions of Eternal Torment* (Chicago: Chicago University Press, 1964).

34. *The Threefold Gift of Christ: By Brother Bernard. Translated and Edited by a Religious of C.M.S.V.* (London: Mowbray & Co., 1954). See Bell, "Bibliography," 120.

CHAPTER TWO

The *Meditationes piisimae*

In this chapter we will be concerned with the content of the *Meditationes*, its author, its sources, and its date. It was the most popular of all the works ever written by or attributed to Bernard of Clairvaux, and according to Robert Bultot, writing in 1964,

> Of the 177 apocryphal writings transmitted under the name of Saint Bernard,[1] the *Meditationes piisimae de cognitione conditionis humanae*, together with the letter *De cura et modo rei familiaris*, are the oldest and most widespread. Several hundred manuscripts, numerous editions, translations into all the major European languages,[2] and continual borrowing from the work clearly attest to its diffusion and influence to the fifteenth century and even beyond.[3]

How many manuscripts survive? It is instructive to compare the number with that of some well-known genuine works of Saint Bernard, the sermons on the Song of Songs, the sermons *De diversis*,

---

1. Bultot is following the list in Leopold Janauschek, *Bibliographia Bernardina* (Vienna: A. Hölder, 1891; repr. Hildesheim: G. Olms, 1959), iv–xiv; see chap. 1, n. 12.

2. Janauschek lists translations in Danish, Dutch/Flemish, English, French, German, Hungarian, Icelandic, Italian, Portuguese, and Swedish; see Janauschek, *Bibliographia Bernardina*, 495–96.

3. Bultot, "Les 'Meditationes,'" 256.

and the *De gradibus humilitatis et superbiae*. The FAMA database created by the *Institut de recherche et d'histoire des textes* (IRHT) in Paris[4] notes about forty-seven, twenty-seven, and seventy-one manuscripts of these three works respectively. And how many for the *Meditationes*? An almost unbelievable 671, and this number is unquestionably incomplete.[5] It is true that not all these manuscripts contain the complete text, but the number remains astonishing.

But for all that, says Bultot, the work has never received the attention it deserves. Bultot attempted to rectify this situation in his lengthy article, and—for the time—did an excellent job. I say "for the time" because the article was published in 1964, which means that the author could not possibly have had access to a personal computer or to any of the multitudinous and essential online resources that are so important in modern research. For Bultot, tracing sources demanded extensive reading and study; nowadays it requires only extensive patience. The first full-length study of the *Meditationes*, or, more accurately, certain aspects of the *Meditationes*, was published in 2016 by Cédric Giraud, who, as we said in chapter one, showed clearly how the Western concept of the nature and practice of meditation was molded by this and other *ps*.-Bernardine texts.[6]

The *Meditationes* are actually part of a small group of related texts that include the *ps*.-Augustinian *De diligendo Deo* (PL 40:847–64),[7] the *De spiritu et anima* (PL 40:779–832), the *Manuale* (PL 40:51–68), the *Soliloquia* (PL 40:863–98), and the *De interiori domo* (or *De conscientia aedificanda*) (PL 184:507C–52C). The most through investigation so far of their inter-relationship has been carried out by Cédric Giraud,[8] but that is not our con-

---

4. Fama.irht.cnrs.fr.

5. See the FAMA list at http://fama.irht.cnrs.fr/oeuvre/267497, supplemented by Giraud, *Spiritualité*, 155–60 and 476. For the printing history of the text, see Giraud, *Spiritualité*, 382–85.

6. See chap. 1, n. 17.

7. Not the *De diligendo Deo* of Bernard.

8. See Giraud, *Spiritualité*, chaps. 2–3.

cern here. Our concern is with the *Meditationes* alone, so let us begin with the title.

It is usually referred to as the *Meditationes piisimae de cognitione conditionis humanae*, "Very Devout Meditations on the Knowledge of the Human Condition." This is the title that appeared in Jean Mabillon's edition of the *opera omnia* of Saint Bernard, first published in 1677 and then reproduced in the pages of volume 184 of the Patrologia Latina edited by Jacques-Paul Migne and published in 1862 (PL 184:485–508). This has now become the customary title by which the work is known, and this edition forms the basis for this present translation. It is not, however, the only title under which the work appears in the manuscript tradition, and both Bultot and Giraud provide a list of many more. That presented by Giraud is the most comprehensive. *Meditationes* and *Tractatus de interiori hominis* are among the most common, but we also have *Meditationes B. Bernardi ad Deum contemplandum, Qualiter ymago Trinitatis in nobis cognosci potest, De contemplatione animae, Compilacio B. Bernardi de gemma animae, Liber B. Bernardi de humana miseria, Speculum animae S. Bernardi, Quomodo per cognitionem nostri venimus ad cognitionem Dei*, and many others.[9]

The work belongs to three over-lapping genres: the *contemptus mundi* literature, the image and likeness literature, and the "Know thyself" literature. As to the first of these, Robert Bultot himself proposed a six-volume study beginning with Ambrose of Milan and ending with the *De miseria conditionis humanae*, "On the Misery of the Human Condition," of Pope Innocent III that we mentioned towards the end of chapter one. So far as I know, only four volumes were ever published,[10] and Bultot died in 1990. As to the second, the magisterial study by Robert Javelet, *Image et resemblance au*

---

9. See Bultot, "Les 'Meditationes,' " 283–84; and Giraud, *Spiritualité*, 157–60. Giraud's summary on page 477 lists thirty-five different titles.

10. The fourth was entitled *La doctrine du mépris du monde en occident, de S. Ambroise à Innocent IIII. Tome IV: Le XIe siècle: Jean de Fécamp, Hermann Contract, Roger de Caen, Anselme de Canterbury* (Paris: Béatrice-Nauwelaerts, 1964).

douzième siècle, published in 1967,[11] remains indispensable, while for the third, we have the three superb volumes by Pierre Courcelle, *Connais-toi toi-même; de Socrate à saint Bernard*, published in 1974–1975.[12] Besides these, there is an immense secondary literature, but these three studies remain fundamental.

We will examine the content of the *Meditationes*, its theory and practice, in more detail in chapters three and four, but for the moment it may be useful to offer a brief summary of the book. The Mabillon/Migne edition is divided into fifteen chapters. The first is an entirely optimistic assessment of our creation to the image and likeness of God, and thus, if we are to know God, how necessary it is that we should know ourselves. The second and most of the third chapters are entirely pessimistic, describing the disgusting nature of the human body, the miseries of our fleeting life in this world, the prevalence of sin, and the ghastly fate that awaits sinners at the Last Day. But chapter three also reminds us of the nobility of the soul, its creation *ad imaginem Dei*, and the need for us to return to our divine homeland. "Take no notice of what the flesh wants, but what the spirit needs" (§9, para. 1), and this, by God's grace, will lead us to the delights of Paradise, culminating in the vision of God himself, that are described in chapter four.

How do we begin this process? By the daily self-examination prescribed in the short fifth chapter, which brings us back to the principle of knowing oneself. But to this must be added attentive prayer—the subject of chapter six—and the guarding of the heart discussed in chapter seven. What the author means by this is keeping control of our thoughts and desires, and directing our heart and mind unswervingly to God and the things that pertain to God. This is no easy task, and both here and in the following chapter, the writers admits that he only occasionally manages to achieve it.

11. Robert Javelet, *Image et ressemblance au douzième siècle de saint Anselme à Alain de Lille* (Paris: Letouzey & Ané, 1967).

12. Pierre Courcelle, *Connais-toi toi-même; de Socrate à saint Bernard* (Paris: Études augustiniennes, 1974–1975)

The essential problem here is the fickle and unstable nature of the human heart, the subject of chapter nine. It busies itself with a multitude of things, running hither and thither at a whim, and, as Augustine says at the very beginning of his *Confessions*, it is restless until it finds rest in God. That we will err and stray, therefore, is inevitable, but happily grace is available to forgive us our sins. This leads the writer, both here and elsewhere, to speak of confession, and that it needs to be complete and sincere if it is to be effective.

Within a monastery, one of the ways in which one's sinfulness is made evident is the Chapter of Faults, where any brother may accuse another of some abuse or infraction of the monastic rule or usages. This is the subject of chapter ten, and the writer admits that he does not care for it. But whether he likes it or not, it is an essential tool in the quest for self-knowledge, for we cannot try to heal diseases that we do not know we have or correct errors that we do not know we committed. On the other hand—we are now at chapter eleven—his conscience knows all these things. It has recorded them all in minute detail and will reveal them all when it comes time for the soul to appear before the Supreme Judge.

Chapters twelve and thirteen deal with the problems of life in the world, and the allurements and temptations of the world, the flesh, and the devil. Life here below is a constant battle against their attacks, and we need all the help we can get. These two chapters are, as we might expect, fairly pessimistic, but they also imbue us with the desire to do all that we can (with God's help) to triumph in these constant battles, so that God, in his mercy, will look kindly upon us and bring us at the end into the delights of Paradise. Chapter fourteen describes the supreme joy of that heavenly homeland and ends, optimistically, by stating that "the more we love God, the more closely shall we see him whom we long to behold."

The final chapter—chapter fifteen—is a brief recapitulation of the whole treatise. The problem lies with the "old self," the *vetus homo* of Ephesians 4:22, which we inherited from Adam and Eve. By that first sin, our likeness to God was lost (though the image remains), and our concern here below is the restoration of the lost likeness. We must therefore know ourselves for what we are, treat those things that are transitory and worldly with contempt, and, with the help of God's grace (and only with the help of God's grace), crucify the old self on the cross of Christ! Then we shall come from darkness into light, from the power of the devil to the hand of the Mediator, and all our sorrows will be turned into joy. Then "after the darkness of this life you may see the first light of the dawning day and see, too, at midday the Sun of Righteousness, in whom you will behold the Bridegroom with the bride, one and the same Lord of Glory, who lives and reigns for endless ages. Amen."[13]

So who was the author of this astonishingly popular little book? It was certainly not Bernard. The style could not be more different, and the only passages in the work that actually come from Bernard are those in which the author is quoting him. But most of the extant manuscripts attribute the treatise to Bernard, though occasionally we also find it attributed to Augustine, Hugh of Saint-Victor, and Innocent III,[14] and by the thirteenth century Bernard's authorship seems to have been generally accepted. A glance at Series A and B of the Brepols *Library of Latin Texts* database shows Bonaventure (d. 1274) and Nicholas of Gorran (d. 1295) attributing it to *Bernardus*, and William of Auvergne (d. 1249) to *beatus Bernardus*. Somewhat later, Bernardino of Siena (d. 1444) also attributes it to *Bernardus*.

But if Bernard did not, in fact, compose the work, who did? We have no idea, though a strong case has been made for Peter Comestor, the author of the *Historia scholastica*, who died at the abbey of Saint-Victor in Paris in 1178 or 1179. This suggestion was first propounded by the learned Maurist Pierre Coustant (1654–1721) (see PL 40:847) and revived by Gaetano Raciti in

---

13. This is the very last sentence of the treatise.
14. See Giraud, *Spiritualité*, 477.

1961.[15] Robert Bultot presents a detailed examination of this hypothesis[16] and concludes that there are weighty arguments against it. In his view, "in the present state of research, the arguments against the attribution take precedence over those in its favour."[17] I agree with Bultot, and, in my own opinion, I do not think there can be any real doubt that the unknown author was a Cistercian. Let us look at the evidence. What can we actually say of the author?

We can say three things. First he is a monk who has a monastic tonsure and wears a cowl.[18] Second, he is certainly a priest, since he serves at the altar, celebrates Mass, and refers to himself as a *sacerdos*.[19] Third, he lives in a monastery and is required to attend the Chapter of Faults.[20] To be a priest-monk is obviously not solely Cistercian, and although the Chapter of Faults was not uniquely Cistercian, in the twelfth century it was, one might say, typically Cistercian.[21] But two other factors need to be taken into account. As Jean Leclercq has said, the *Meditationes* remains faithful to the ideas of Saint Bernard, though in his view they were probably written one or more generations after him.[22] And although some of the few authors who have discussed the *Meditationes* have not wholly discounted a Victorine or Cluniac origin,[23] the majority opinion is that it came from a Cistercian milieu. This is supported, I would suggest, by one final factor: that of the writer's sources.

15. See Gaetano Raciti, "L'autore del 'De spiritu et anima,'" *Rivista di Filosofia Neo-Scolastica* 53 (1961): 385–401.

16. See Bultot, "Les 'Meditationes,'" 287–92.

17. Bultot, "Les 'Meditationes,'" 292.

18. See n. 253 to the translation.

19. See n. 150 to the translation.

20. See n. 233 to the translation.

21. The Chapter of Faults will be discussed in more detail in chap. 4.

22. See Jean Leclercq, "Études sur saint Bernard et le texte de ses écrits," *Analecta Sacri Ordinis Cisterciensis* 9 (1953): 37.

23. See Bultot, "Les 'Meditationes,'" 257–58, 283. Bultot himself rejects a Cluniac origin and is very doubtful with regard to a Victorine. See also Giraud, *Spiritualité*, 168–69.

In 1964, Robert Bultot did a fine job of tracing a number of these sources, but, as we said above, he obviously did not have available to him the electronic tools that we have today. He certainly demonstrates the importance of Augustine and Bernard in the composition of the treatise, but there is considerably more to be said. So before we go further in identifying the order to which the writer belonged, we must turn our attention to the sources he used.

The task of Robert Bultot was not made any easier by the skill with which the little book is put together. It cannot be called a florilegium. It may, perhaps, be called a pastiche, but the various sections flow together seamlessly, and the whole is greater than its various parts. Nowhere do we find, as we find in so many other writers, *sicut dicit beatus Augustinus*, "as blessed Augustine says," or blessed Bernard, or blessed anyone else. In fact, there are but three names mentioned in the whole of the treatise, those of Saint Paul, Saint James, and the prophet Hosea, which is not a great deal of help. Fortunately, and thanks to the library resources of Memorial University here in Newfoundland, I have at my disposal the Chadwyck-Healey Patrologia Latina database with its wonderful search tools, and all the databases made available online by Brepols (primarily the two series of the *Library of Latin Texts*).

In 1911, Henry Osborn Taylor referred to the tracing of sources as "an affair of dull diligence,"[24] and although there is some truth in this, it is not the whole truth. Tracing sources using modern databases may, perhaps, be likened to fly fishing, though I am not a fisherman. You cast your line into the pond or river time after time with no bite, but then, finally, your patience is rewarded and you are granted your just reward. It may be no more than a minnow, or it may be a splendid trout. Tracing sources is similar, especially with a writer like the author of the *Meditationes*. He will take a source, sometimes a substantial source, quote some parts of it verbatim, but paraphrase others. He will also make omissions

---

24. Henry Osborn Taylor, *The Mediaeval Mind: A History of the Development of Thought and Emotion in the Middle Ages,* 2 vols. (London: Macmillan & Co., 1911), 2:148.

and has no hesitation in adding material, though not usually in any great quantity. What this means is that the search engine may not pick up a phrase from, say, Augustine, because the author has made a minor adjustment to that phrase, even if it is no more than *aut* for *vel*. What I had to do, therefore, was to choose the most unusual words and check the occurrence and context of each one of them in the Patrologia Latina. Unfortunately, unusual words are not overabundant in the *Meditationes*, and it was often a case of taking a couple of common words and using the tools provided by the search engines to see if they could be traced. Sometimes I checked almost every word in a column before catching my fish. Sometimes it was a very small fish—three words from Richard of Saint-Victor, which we will discuss in a moment— but sometimes it was a very big fish indeed. The whole of §26 in chapter nine, for example, is directly dependent on the *De sacramentis christianae fidei* of Hugh of Saint-Victor. I suppose this could be described as an affair of dull diligence—it certainly took a great deal of patience—but it was also very rewarding. So what were the sources used by the author of the *Meditationes*?[25]

As we said above, Bultot, without the befit of these databases, was able to identify a number of passages, primarily from Augustine and Bernard, on which the author was dependent, and Cédric Giraud added a few more.[26] There remained, however, many more to be discovered, and although I am quite certain I have still missed some, I hope I have not missed too many.

Here, then, is a list in alphabetical order of all the sources so far traced. Those with a question mark are doubtful and will be discussed in due course: Adam of Saint-Victor?, Ambrose of Milan, Anselm and *ps.*-Anselm of Canterbury, Arnold of Bonneval, Augustine and *ps.*-Augustine, Bede the Venerable, Bernard of Clairvaux, Boethius, Cassiodorus, Claudianus Mamertus, Gregory and *ps.*-Gregory the Great, Guigo I of la Chartreuse, Hildebert of

---

25. For details, see the *Index of Patristic and Medieval Sources* at the end of this volume. What follows here is based on that list.

26. See Giraud, *Spiritualité*, 163–70.

Lavardin, Hugh and *ps.*-Hugh of Saint-Victor, Isidore of Seville, Jerome, John Cassian, *ps.*-Julian of Toledo, Lawrence of Novara?, Odo of Cluny, Ouen (Audoenus) of Rouen?, Peter Damian, Rabanus Maurus, *Regula ad virgines, Regula S. Benedicti*, Richard of Saint-Victor, Seneca the Younger, and Pope Sixtus II. It is a formidable list. How many of these sources the author actually read, or how many of them he found in florilegia, we do not know.

Of these, by far the greatest number come from Augustine (with *ps.*-Augustine) and Bernard. How many? There are eighteen passages from the authentic writings of Augustine, eight from *ps.*-Augustine, and no fewer than twenty-two from Bernard of Clairvaux. The Augustinian passages come primarily from the *De civitate Dei* and *De Trinitate* (they account for twelve of them), and the most important of the *ps.*-Augustinian sources is the *De rectitudine catholicae conversationis* (PL 40:1169–90), to which we shall return in a moment. The Bernardine sources are more diverse. The sermons predominate, mainly the sermons *de tempore*, but also passages from six of the sermons *de diversis*. There is not a great deal from the sermons on the Song of Songs, but as we said earlier, there is no Bernardine mysticism in the *Meditationes*. Nor is there any mention of the Virgin Mary, and a passage that has been much influenced by Bernard's second sermon for the feast of the Assumption deals with confession, not the Mother of God.[27] There are also passages from four different letters. So far as I have been able to tell, Bernard is the only Cistercian source for the *Meditationes*. I have not been able to identify anything from (for example) Guerric of Igny, William of Saint-Thierry, Gilbert of Hoyland, and certainly not Isaac of Stella. C. H. Talbot suggested Aelred of Rievaulx as the source of one passage,[28] but Bultot effectively dismisses this, and I agree with Bultot.[29]

27. See n. 228 to the translation.

28. Charles H. Talbot, "The *Speculum humilitatis* attributed to Ailred of Rievaulx," *Studia Monastica* 1 (1959): 126.

29. See Bultot, "Les 'Meditationes,'" 282, n. 43.

After Bernard and Augustine, there is a long gap before we come to Gregory the Great, who is represented by six passages, and Hugh of Saint-Victor, who is represented by five. The Gregorian passages are taken from the *Moralia* on the book of Job (no surprise here: the *Moralia* were read in the refectory of Cistercian houses), his homilies on Ezekiel and the gospels, and a single passage from the *Pastoral Rule*. As to Hugh, there are two passages from his *De sacramentis*, and one each from the *De institutione novitiorum*, the *Didascalicon*, and the *Summa sententiarum*. Then come Isidore of Seville, represented by four passages, and Hildebert of Lavardin, represented by three. All the others in the list contribute just one or two passages, and although most of the names are not uncommon, some are a little more unusual. Ambrose, Anselm of Canterbury, Bede, Cassiodorus, Claudianus Mamerus, Jerome, John Cassian, Peter Damian, Rabanus Maurus, and, of course, the Rule of Saint Benedict may not surprise us, but it is interesting to find passages from Arnold of Bonneval, Guigo I of la Chartreuse, and Odo of Cluny. Arnold contributes a passage from his *De operibus sex dierum* and Guigo from his *Meditationes*, and from Odo come two selections from his *Collationes*. The passages from the commentary on Nahum attributed, incorrectly, to Julian of Toledo are less unusual than they may at first appear: the work was widely circulated.

But what of Ouen of Rouen's life of Saint Eligius of Noyon? This is a little tricky. There are two passages here,[30] and both of them appear in identical form in two works, the life of Saint Eligius and the *ps.*-Augustinian *De rectitudine catholicae conversationis*. The two works are, in fact, related,[31] and the *De rectitudine* also appears under the name of Eligius himself. To make matters even more complicated, it is by no means certain that Ouen or Audoenus, who died in 684, actually wrote the life of Eligius, who had died more than twenty years earlier in 660. In short,

30. See nn. 57 and 101 to the translation.
31. See the important notes in CPL nos. 2094 and 2096.

since we are quite uncertain as to the authorship of both of these works, we are equally uncertain as to their date, and to launch into a full investigation of this complex problem would take us far off track. Whatever the facts of the matter, it may be that these texts attributed to Ouen and Eligius may indicate that the author of the *Meditationes* had a Rouen connection, which might possibly indicate the abbeys of Beaubec, Foucarmont, or Mortemer. But it need hardly be added that this is rank speculation.

The two other questionable sources in the list are Adam of Saint-Victor and Lawrence of Novara. It was Robert Bultot who suggested Adam of Saint-Victor, and to understand this we need to say something about the poetry in the *Meditationes*. The text is unusual in that, unlike the other *ps.*-Bernardine works, it contains a number of passages in verse, ranging from one line to four. Exactly how many there are is unclear since not all of them appear in all manuscripts, and Bultot has suggested that some of them may have been added by a later copyist, or were perhaps marginal additions by later readers that somehow became incorporated into the text.[32] In the Mabillon/Migne edition there are eleven such passages, and one of them reads as follows:

> *Post hominem vermis, post vermem fetor et horror.*
> *Sic in non hominem vertitur omnis homo.*

> "After the human the worm. After the worm, stench and
> horror.
> Thus is each person turned into a non-person."[33]

In this precise form, this distich is not recorded in any of the standard databases and appears nowhere else in the pages of the Migne Patrology. Bultot, however, draws attention to a line from the epitaph for Adam of Saint-Victor that reads *Post hominem vermis, post vermem fit cinis, heu! heu!*, "After the human the

32. Bultot, "Les 'Meditationes,'" 274–75. This is where we desperately need a critical edition.

33. See n. 73 to the translation.

worm, after the worm he becomes ashes, alas! alas!"[34] I am not persuaded by Bultot's argument. The sentiment was well known, and similar passages are common. That Hugh of Saint-Victor was a source for the author of the *Meditationes* is not in doubt; I would not include Adam.[35] The question of Richard we shall discuss in a moment. So what of Lawrence of Novara?

We are speaking here of a charming passage in the *Meditationes* that deals with prayer:

> Wherever you may be, then, pray within yourself. If you are far from a place of prayer, don't look for a place, because you yourself are the place! If you're in bed or anywhere else, pray, and there's your temple! (§17)[36]

Here now is a very similar passage from the sermon *de muliere Chananaea*, "On the Canaanite woman" (see Matt 15:22), attributed to Lawrence, who was an early fifth-century bishop of Novara:[37]

> What, then, if you are in a public place? Pray within yourself. Don't look for a place [to pray]: you yourself are the place! If you're in the bath, pray, and there's your temple.[38]

It is true that *ps.*-Bernard changed the public place into an oratory and the bath into a bed, but the similarities are surely too great for coincidence. The problem is the authorship of the *de muliere*

34. Bultot, "Les 'Meditationes,'" 277.

35. Giraude, *Spiritualité*, 164, n. 148, draws attention to a passage from the *De octo vitiis* of Bernard of Cluny, but although the sentiment is similar, I cannot see it as a source.

36. PL 184:496CD: *Si longe fueris ab oratorio, noli quaerere locum, quoniam tu ipse locus es. Si fueris in lecto aut in alio loco, ora, et ibi est templum.*

37. On Lawrence, see CPL nos. 644–45.

38. Lawrence of Novara?, *De muliere Chananaea*; PL 66:123AB: *Quid ergo si fueris in publico foro? ora intra te: noli quaerere locum; locus ipse es. Ibi, ubi fueris, ora. Si fueris in balneo, ora, et ibi templum est.*

Chananaea. What seems most probable is that the sermon was originally the work of John Chrysostom and was translated into Latin by Bishop Lawrence, but that cannot be regarded as certain.[39] I was not quite certain, therefore, whether to list John Chrysostom as one of *ps.*-Bernard's sources, or Lawrence of Novara. I chose Lawrence since the little treatise normally circulated under his name and was widely read.

As to classical authors, I have been able to trace only one, namely, Seneca the Younger, whose Moral Letters to Lucilius were well known and very popular. He is quoted twice and paraphrased once. In one case, however, it is fairly certain that *ps.*-Bernard has taken the quotation from one of Bernard's genuine sermons *de diversis.*[40] In the other case, the line quoted—*Omnis siquidem res aliena est a nobis: tempus autem tantum nostrum est,* "All things are foreign to us: only time is our own."—does not appear in this form anywhere else in the Patrologia Latina, nor in any of the other databases, save for those that attribute it directly to Seneca. It was, however, a well-known proverbial saying. As to the paraphrase, this echoes another well-known dictum of Seneca: "It is uncertain in what place death awaits you, so await it in every place," which appears in exactly this form in the last chapter of the *ps.*-Augustinian *Formula honestae vitae.*[41] I very much doubt that *ps.*-Bernard had actually been reading Seneca. The question of Boethius will be discussed in the next chapter.

So after this long excursus on *ps.*-Bernard's sources, what can we say about the order to which he belonged? The points we have already mentioned—the monk-priest, attendance at the Chapter of Faults, and the fact that the text of the *Meditationes* remains faithful to the ideas of Saint Bernard—do not in themselves prove that he was Cistercian, and Cédric Giraud sees no reason why

39. See the discussion in CPL no. 645.
40. See n. 252 to the translation.
41. See n. 98 to the translation.

he should not have been a Benedictine,[42] but when we look at the dominant position held by Bernard in the sources used by the author, together with the fact that from the earliest times the treatise has been attributed to Bernard, then what I would suggest is that while none of them taken individually proves a Cistercian origin, taken collectively they leave us in little doubt on the matter. Bonaventure and William of Auvergne and Nicholas of Gorran might have gotten the author of the work wrong, but they were right about his order.

So what is the date of the work? To help us in this we must return once again to the list of sources. This includes a number of eleventh/twelfth-century writers—Arnold of Bonneval, Bernard himself, Guigo I, Hildebert, Hugh of Saint-Victor—but the latest of them appears to be Richard of Saint-Victor. I say "appears to be," because my identification of Richard as a source is dependent on three words alone. In §16 of chapter six, *ps.*-Bernard tells his friend that when he goes into a church to praise God, he should leave "the tumult of his ever-changing thoughts" and all his worldly cares outside so that he can be free for God alone. The Latin here reads *fluctuantium cogitationum tumultus*, and the only other place that this appears in the Patrologia Latina is in Richard's *Benjamin major*.[43] I am quite aware that this is a tenuous identification, and I can find no trace of Richard anywhere else in the *Meditationes*. If the author has indeed taken this from Richard, and since Richard died in March 1173, and since there is no hint of the Schools in the work, it would suggest a date of composition sometime in the last quarter of the twelfth century. Jean Leclercq, as we saw above, suggested that the author was writing "one or more generations after Bernard,"[44] but if *fluctuantium cogitationum tumultus* is no more

---

42. See Giraud, *Spiritualité*, 168–69.

43. See n. 158 to the translation. *Cogitationum* with some form of *tumultus* is common, but with the addition of *fluctuantium* it is very rare. I searched the PL using all the tools available to me.

44. See n. 22 above, and Bultot, "Les 'Meditationes,' " 258–59.

than an astonishing coincidence, then all we can say is that the treatise was composed sometime in the period between the death of Bernard in 1153 and a date prior to the end of the twelfth century. It is certainly not a thirteenth-century work. My own suggestion would be sometime between 1170 and 1190—Giraud prefers 1160 to 1190[45]—and I would adduce one more piece of evidence in support of this hypothesis.

There exists an extremely long commentary on the Song of Songs by Thomas of Perseigne on which, in the past, I have published a number of studies. It is dedicated *Reverendo Patri domino Pontio, Dei gratia Clarmontensi episcopo* (PL 206:17A), that is to say, to the Cistercian Pontius (Pons) de Polignac, abbot of Clairvaux from 1165 to 1170, and bishop of Clermont from 1170 to his death in 1189. It was a very popular work—there are almost ninety surviving manuscripts[46]—and exhibits a number of interesting features. Two of these are of importance to us here. One is the way in which this mammoth commentary weaves together a multitude of sources to form a collective whole that reads easily. The other is the effortless way in which Thomas fuses together Cistercian and Victorine spirituality. In 1977, in my first study of Thomas's commentary, I made the comment that "we may conclude, therefore, that by the end of the twelfth century, we can no longer speak (if we ever could) of a specifically Cistercian and specifically Victorine spirituality. There is too large a degree of overlap."[47]

This is just what we have in the *ps.*-Bernardine *Meditationes*. There is a multitude of sources, seamlessly woven together, and a spirituality that, while predominantly that of Bernard, well reflects

45. Giraud, *Spiritualité*, 170.

46. See David N. Bell, "Le Commentaire du Cantique des Cantiques de Thomas de Perseigne Revisité," *Annales de Bretagne et des Pays de l'Ouest* 120 (2013): 117–31, here 129.

47. David N. Bell, "The Commentary on the Song of Songs of Thomas the Cistercian and His Conception of the Image of God," *Cîteaux—Commentarii cistercienses* 28 (1977): 5–25, here 24. See also Bell, "Le Commentaire du Cantique des Cantiques," 117–18.

the strong influence of Hugh of Saint-Victor. Thomas's commentary must date from any time between 1170 and 1189, and that is my own opinion as to the date of the *Meditationes*.

So let us now summarize our conclusions in this first chapter. There are five points. First, as may be seen from the huge number of surviving manuscripts and translation into all the major European languages, the *ps.*-Bernardine *Meditationes* were immensely popular and read everywhere. Second, their content is spiritual and pastoral, but not mystical. The purpose of the book is to instill in the reader a contempt for the world and worldly things, to arouse a desire and an intention to restore the lost likeness and let the image of God shine forth once again, to give guidance in self-examination, prayer, confession, and other practices that may assist us in this, and to describe the glories and joys of Paradise, where, when we die, God and his angels wish us to be. Mystical union with God here on earth is not mentioned at all. Third, we have no idea of the identity of the author. The case for Peter Comestor will not bear close scrutiny, and all that we can say is that he was a monk-priest, almost certainly (I would say certainly) Cistercian. We have no idea of his monastery, and the Rouen connection is so tenuous that I hesitate to mention it. Fourth, whoever he was, he had access to a good library and had read a great deal. The list of his sources is impressive, but almost half of all the passages identified are taken from Augustine or *ps.*-Augustine and Bernard. And finally, as to the date of the work, I would suggest that the evidence points to the period sometime between about 1170 and 1190, much the same date as the long commentary on the Song of Songs of Thomas of Perseigne, with which the far briefer *Meditationes* shares a number of important characteristics.

Earlier in this chapter, we presented a brief summary of the content of the work, but it is now time to examine this in more detail and, especially, to provide some background to the theory and practice expressed in the treatise so as to help anyone who reads it to understand it better.

CHAPTER THREE

The Teaching of the *Meditationes*: Theory

The purpose of the next two chapters is not to present a summary of the *Meditationes*. That has already been done in chapter one, and the whole brief text appears in English translation in the second part of this book. My purpose here is to present certain materials that may act as a background to the work, a foundation to help in understanding where the author is coming from, and where the text stands in the religious, theological, and spiritual context of the times.

The *Meditationes* has three themes: our creation *ad imaginem Dei*, our fallen human nature, and practical instruction as to how we can restore the lost likeness. There is nothing new in any of this.[1] What is new is the way in which the unknown author takes a variety of sources and weaves them together to form a cohesive whole but yet retains his own personality. By the third sentence of the treatise he is already quoting Augustine's *De Trinitate*, and the figures of Augustine and Bernard dominate the work.

Augustine's doctrine of the Trinity differed from that of the Greek East. In the East, the theologians saw the Father as the fountainhead of deity who eternally begets the Son and then, through

---

1. See *Three Treatises on Man: A Cistercian Anthropology*, ed. Bernard McGinn, CF 24 (Kalamazoo, MI: Cistercian Publications, 1977), 75–93.

the Son, puts forth the Holy Spirit. Elsewhere I have likened this to the water in a reservoir (the Father) being channelled through pipes (the Son) to the faucets on our own sinks (the Holy Spirit). The Holy Spirit, therefore, proceeds (the verb is borrowed from John 15:26) *from* the Father *through* the Son, and the technical theological term for this is Single Procession.[2]

Augustine's view was radically different. For him, the Father eternally begets the Son, but then both Father and Son together put forth the Holy Spirit. Using an anachronistic analogy, it is similar to a car battery. There are two terminals, positive and negative, and if we lead a wire from each and touch the ends of the wires together, we get a spark. That's the Holy Spirit: the mutual interaction of Father and Son. And Augustine defines the Holy Spirit as the mutual love of Father and Son, the love that proceeds from them both and that is common to both.[3] The Spirit is, in fact, whatever is common to Father and Son, whatever that may be: their mutual communion, for example, or their mutual will, charity, joy, happiness, blessedness, goodness, and so on.[4] And since, in this case, the Holy Spirit proceeds from the Father and the Son, this is referred to technically as Double Procession. We can actually see traces of the doctrine prior to Augustine, in Jerome and Ambrose of Milan, for example, and even in the Greek East in the writings of Cyril of Alexandria, but it was Augustine who perfected it.

Above all, the Holy Spirit is the mutual love and will of Father and Son, and for Augustine, love and will are the same thing. But we must be careful with our terminology here. In Latin there are

2. See David N. Bell, *A Cloud of Witnesses: An Introduction to the Development of Christian Doctrine to AD 500*, CS 218, 2nd ed. (Kalamazoo, MI: Cistercian Publications, 2007), 97–101.

3. See especially Augustine, *De Trinitate* XV.xvii.27; PL 42:1079–80, and XV.vi.10; PL 42:1064.

4. See David N. Bell, *The Image and Likeness: The Augustinian Spirituality of William of St Thierry*, CS 78 (Kalamazoo, MI: Cistercian Publications, 1984), 57–58, for all these terms and references to Augustine.

three words for love: *amor*, *dilectio*, and *caritas*, love, dilection, and charity in English, though the word *dilection* is now obsolete. *Amor* is the generic or neutral term for love, and may refer to all forms of love, good or bad, properly directed or misdirected, spiritual or carnal. *Caritas*, on the other hand, always refers to love that is properly directed, and Augustine provides an exact definition: "I call charity a movement of the soul towards the enjoyment of God [*ad fruendum Deo*] for his own sake, and of oneself and one's neighbor for the sake of God."[5] Charity is one of the three Theological Virtues (the other two being faith and hope), and Saint Paul provides a precise description of its nature in 1 Corinthians 13:4-8. In English, charity normally implies some sort of almsgiving, but that is never the usage in any of the texts we are discussing. It is best, therefore, to translate *caritas* as *charity* even if it sometimes looks a little odd.

Dilectio is sort of in between *amor* and *caritas*, and although it is possible to find it used of carnal love, such usage is very rare. According to Augustine, "All love [*dilectio*], whether it be carnal (which should not be called *dilectio* but rather *amor*, for the term *dilectio* is normally used of better things and understood of better things), all love [*dilectio*], my dearest brothers, certainly involves good will to those who are loved."[6] *Dilectio*, then is almost always used for love in a good sense, but it is a less specific and more all-embracing term than *caritas*. In the Vulgate text of 1 John 4:16, God is *caritas*. In Augustine's version of 1 John, God is *dilectio*. We shall find these distinctions in the *Meditationes*.

As to love and will, the one is no more and no less than an intense form of the other. Love is a directed form of will. It is not something you fall into, but something you cultivate and develop. It is not a warm fuzzy emotional enthrallment, but the laser-beam of the focused will. As Augustine says in his *De Trinitate*, *valentior est voluntas*: love is a stronger, more intense, more vigorous

---

5. Augustine, *De doctrina Christiana*, 3.16; PL 34:72.
6. Augustine, *In epistolam Joannis ad Parthos, tract.* 8.5; PL 35:2038.

form of will.[7] William of Saint-Thierry, who takes up this theme, calls it "vehement will"[8] or "a vehement well-ordered will,"[9] and the author of the *Meditationes* refers to love as *excellentior voluntas*,[10] an expression that appears to be unique to *ps.*-Bernard. But most important, love is both the gift of the Holy Spirit and the Holy Spirit itself, and if we have received that gift, we may use that gift to help us in restoring the lost likeness. How? Because since love and will are the same thing, loving God means uniting our will to God, and that means overcoming that self-will, that egocentricity, that brought about our fall in the first place. "The more we love God," says *ps.*-Bernard, "the more closely shall we see him whom we long to behold" (§37, last line).

But if we are created *ad imaginem Dei*, then where can that image be seen? Since God is eternal and without shape or form, it is certainly not in our human bodies, but in that part of us that, like God, is also eternal and without shape or form, namely, the soul. Once again, there are in Latin three words for soul, *anima, animus,* and *spiritus*, and it is not easy, when translating into English, to distinguish between the first two. A number of twelfth-century Cistercians have much to say on the *anima/animus* distinction— William of Saint-Thierry is a good example—and since *anima* is a feminine noun in Latin and *animus* masculine, what they have to say inevitably reflects twelfth-century views of women and the female gender and is not always appealing to out modern ears. There is nothing of this in the *Meditationes*. The invariable term

7. Augustine, *De Trinitate*, XV.xxi.41; PL 42:1089. See also *De civitate Dei*, XIV.vii.2; PL 41:410; and Étienne Gilson, *The Christian Philosophy of Saint Augustine,* trans. L. E. M. Lynch (New York: Random House, 1967), 134–35.

8. William of Saint-Thierry, *Meditativae orationes*, XII.20; CCCM 89:76; and *Speculum fidei*, 19; CCCM 89A:89, defines *amor* as *uehemens uoluntas*. *De natura et dignitate amoris*, 4; CCCM 88:180, defines it as *uehemens in bono uoluntas.*

9. William of Saint-Thierry, *De contemplando Deo*, 14; CCCM 88:162–63: *Nichil enim aliud est amor, quam uehemens et bene ordinata uoluntas.*

10. See n. 38 to the translation.

for soul is *anima*, and there is, in fact, but one instance in the whole work of the use of the term *animus*, and that in a passage that appears to be original and not borrowed.[11]

It is not just in the soul, however, that the image of God is to be found, but in the *mens* or mind, the highest part of the soul, that part that distinguishes us from any of the animals and makes us just a little lower than the angels. This is standard teaching. And just as there are three persons who operate inseparably in the one united Trinity, so there are three factors that operate inseparably in the human mind. They are, of course, as Augustine made eminently clear in his *De Trinitate,* memory, understanding, and will or love. Augustine actually suggested a considerable number of these Trinitarian analogies,[12] but this one is the best known and certainly the most important. *Ps.*-Bernard (and almost everyone else) is more than happy to take it over. The principle is simple. If I wish to pick up a book, I must remember what a book is, understand the process of picking it up, and have the will to put that process into action. In other words, the single act of picking up the book demands the use of three rational faculties working inseparably, and we may see in this a distant, a very distant, image of the Trinity itself.

Augustine usually speaks of *memoria, intellectus,* and *voluntas/ amor,* but on a few occasions he replaces *intellectus* with *intelligentia.*[13] But *ps.*-Bernard clearly prefers *intelligentia,* and in the four places where he speaks of the trinitarian analogy of memory, understanding, and will, this is the word he uses. *Intellectus* appears only four times in the *Meditationes,* and never as part of the Trinitarian analogy. This may be chance, but I doubt it. I think it

11. See n. 184 to the translation.

12. For a complete list, see Olivier du Roy, *L'intelligence de la foi en la Trinité selon saint Augustin: Genèse de sa théologie trinitaire jusqu'en 391* (Paris: Études augustiniennes, 1966), 537–40.

13. See Augustine, *De Trinitate*, X.xi.17 and 18; PL 42:982, 983; *Ep.* 169. ii.6 to Evodius; PL 33:745.

more likely that it reflects the influence of Boethius, though not necessarily directly. In the *De consolatione philosophiae*, Boethius lists the four powers of the soul as the senses, imagination, reason, and *intelligentia* and states that, as a consequence, we can consider human beings in four different ways.

The senses can examine the human form only as it exists in matter, in its physical form. The imagination can go further than this and judge the appearance of a human being without any material substance, namely, in thought. Reason goes further still and can contemplate the universal aspects of humanity that are contained in specific individuals. But "higher still is the eye of the intelligence, for it transcends the sphere of the [material] universe and, with the pure vision of the mind, gazes on the [Neo-Platonic] Idea [of humanity] in its absolute simplicity."[14] *Intelligentia*, therefore, stands higher than *intellectus*, and provides us with the possibility of the direct perception of ultimate realities.

By memory, says *ps*.-Bernard, one brings God to mind. By understanding, one considers what God is in himself, in the angels, in the saints, in created things, and in human beings. And by love and will, one loves the one who created the writer's soul in his image: "There is nothing so similar to that Supreme Wisdom as the rational mind, which, by memory, understanding, and will, dwells in that ineffable Trinity; nor can it dwell therein unless it remembers it, understands it, and loves it" (§2).[15] Thus, since memory is the repository of all that we know, understanding the process by which we select what is good and true from this, and will the longing to possess those things that are good and true, then "by memory we are like the Father; by understanding like the Son, and by will, like the Holy Spirit" (§3), and the Holy Spirit, the mutual

---

14. Boethius, *De consolatione philosophiae*, V, prosa 4; PL 63:0849AB: *Intelligentiae vero celsior oculus existit. Supergressa namque universitatis ambitum, ipsam illam simplicem formam pura menti acie contuetur.* We are in the world of solid Boethean Neo-Platonism here.

15. *Ps*.-Bernard is quoting Augustine: see n. 23 to the translation.

love of Father and Son, is the key to our achieving the knowledge of God and ourselves. How? Because "love, which is from God and is God, is properly called the Holy Spirit, through whom the charity of God is poured forth in our hearts [Rom 5:5], through whom the whole Trinity dwells within us" (§3, last sentence).

Ps.-Bernard never says that memory *is* the Father and so on, and in this he follows Augustine, who is eminently clear on the point: "I do *not* say 'the Father is memory, the Son is understanding, the Spirit is will'; I do not say this—understand it as you may—I do not venture [to assert it]."[16] The thought of *ps.*-Bernard is similar to that of William of Saint-Thierry: "In order for the rational soul to cleave to God, the Father has claimed [*vindicavit*] memory for himself, the Son reason, and the Holy Spirit will,"[17] but I have found no trace of William himself anywhere in the *Meditationes*.

We should note here that despite the major importance of the genuine Bernard in the *Meditationes*, *ps.*-Bernard's doctrine of the image of God is that of Augustine, not that of Bernard. If I may quote Étienne Gilson,

> In full accord with St. Augustine, St Bernard places the image of God in the mind of man, *mens*; but while Augustine seeks for preference in intellectual cognition where the Divine illumination attests the continuous presence of the Creator to the creature, St. Bernard puts it rather in the will, and very especially in freedom.[18]

This is not the view of the author of the *Meditationes*. The terms free will or free choice, or anything like them, appear nowhere in the work, and *ps.*-Bernard remains solidly aligned with Augustine of Hippo.

---

16. Augustine, *Sermo* 52.x.23; PL 38:364.

17. William of Saint-Thierry, *De natura et dignitate amoris*, 3; CCCM 88:180.

18. Étienne Gilson, trans. A. H. C. Downes, *The Mystical Theology of Saint Bernard* (London & New York: Sheed and Ward; repr. Kalamazoo, MI: Cistercian Publications, 1990), 46. See also pp. 49 and 236, n. 124.

Our creation *ad imaginem et similitudinem Dei* is not only a statement, but also a demand. We are indeed images of God, but, through sin, we have lost the likeness. We have fallen into the *regio dissimilitudinis*, the region of unlikeness, a term used by a multitude of writers (including Augustine and Bernard),[19] but never by the author of the *Meditationes*. The preposition *ad* "to" in the phrase *ad imaginem et similitudinem Dei* implies a process, a demand that we do something about our present wretched condition, and, with God's help, try to restore what we have lost. The theory as to how this is done is simple; the practice is infinitely difficult. We must turn our attention from the things of this world to the things above. "Let me return," says *ps.*-Bernard (quoting Augustine), "from what is outward to what is inward, and let me rise from what is lower to what is higher, so that I might know whence I come and whither I go" (§1). And to goad us to take the necessary steps to this end, *ps.*-Bernard spends a considerable amount of time describing the miseries of the world, the disgusting nature of human bodies, and the lure of worldly pleasures and worldly delights.

This is the *contemptus mundi* tradition, "contempt for the world," examined so thoroughly by Robert Bultot.[20] It has its origins in classical times, but by the twelfth century was a standard part of the Christian ascetic tradition. One of its most dramatic representatives is the long poem *De contemptu mundi*: by Bernard of Cluny,[21] which contrasts the passing pleasures of the world with the eternal joys of heaven. Bernard levies vicious attacks on all the vices and follies of his age, and spares no one. There is, however, a problem with this literature, a problem that stems from Genesis

19. Robert Javelet, *Image et ressemblance au douzième siècle de saint Anselme à Alain de Lille,* 2 vols. (Paris: Letouzey & Ané, 1967), 1:266–85.

20. Robert Bultot, *La doctrine du mépris du monde en occident, de S. Ambroise à Innocent III* (Paris: Éditions Béatrice-Nauwelaerts, 1963–1964). Six volumes were projected, but Bultot died before completing them.

21. Bernardus Morlanensis, *De contemptu mundi, Une vision du monde vers 1144,* Témoins de notre histoire (Turnhout: Brepols, 2009). Latin text with French translation, introduction, and commentary by André Cresson.

1:31, a verse that tells us that after the seventh day of creation, God saw all the things he had made "and they were very good." But if there is nothing wrong or evil about the created order, what justification can we have for despising it? And since human beings are part of the created order, what's wrong with the flesh?

The answer, of course, is that there is nothing intrinsically evil about creation: everything depends on how we use it. There is nothing intrinsically evil about gunpowder, but some people use it to blow up others, and some people use it to make fireworks. Similarly, there is nothing intrinsically evil about the flesh—I mean the actual physical substance of the flesh—but its nature has been affected by the Fall, and the soul that animates it has been stained and corrupted.

Both Eastern and Western theologians agreed that before the Fall, Adam and Eve were in a state of blessedness and perfection. They could talk freely with God, all their wants were satisfied in Eden, and had they not sinned, they would not have died. Unfortunately, they did sin, and as a consequence of that first sin they became mortal, susceptible to disease and corruption, and their souls were stained or corrupted. And both Eastern and Western theologians agreed that this taint, this stain, was passed down from Adam and Eve to their descendants—i.e., us—and that ever since Adam and Eve were expelled from the Garden of Eden, the whole human race has been born mortal, sinful, and liable to disease and corruption.

The Eastern theologians, however, never thought that this corruption was absolute. That is to say, they never thought that as a consequence of the Fall, human beings had entirely lost the ability to do good. They had certainly lost the ability to do enough good, by their own strength, to achieve salvation—for that, grace was essential—but they were still capable of good actions. If, then, they did a good action, God would respond to this by making his grace available to them, and then in cooperation with this grace they could do more good actions. Thus, in cooperation with grace, and only in cooperation with grace, they might achieve salvation.

On the whole, this was also the view of Western theologians up to the time of Augustine. His view was radically different and came about as a result of his conflict with a British ascetic named Pelagius, who maintained that souls came into this world absolutely pure and quite untainted by any sin of Adam and Eve. Those interested can read the details elsewhere,[22] but Augustine had no time at all for the views of Pelagius. As a result of a misreading of Romans 5:12, he maintained not only that human beings were innately corrupted, but that that corruption was total. The verse in question reads, in Greek, "Through one man sin entered this world, and through sin, death; and thus death passed on to all people because all sinned." But in the Latin translation used by Augustine, the Greek for "because" in the phrase for "because all sinned" was rendered into Latin as *in quo*, which, unfortunately, can have two meanings. The first is "in that," which is the same as "because," and is what the original Greek says. The second is "in whom," and that is how Augustine read it. In other words, since the whole human race was present in potentiality in Adam, whatever Adam did, we did, and when Adam was tempted and fell, we fell with him. Thus, since we all fell "in Adam," so we are what Adam was: fallen, damned, guilty, and condemned.

In other words, the newly created soul was not only stained, but 100% stained, and, as a consequence, human beings come into this world utterly incapable of performing a single good action, any more than a perfectly dark room could emit a beam of light. As Augustine said, "Of our own power, we can only fall."[23] This idea leads ineluctably to the doctrine of predestination and a variety of problems that are not here our concern.[24] But in the West, the immense authority of Augustine led to this pessimistic

22. See David N. Bell, *A Cloud of Witnesses: An Introductory History of the Development of Christian Doctrine,* CS 109 (Kalamazoo, MI: Cistercian Publications, 1989), 155–61.

23. Augustine, *Enarratio in Ps.* 129.1; PL 37:1696.

24. For a discussion, see Bell, *Cloud of Witnesses*, 158–65.

doctrine being universally accepted, and by the twelfth century, only the most determined heretics would dare to question it. In short, as far as the West was concerned, the Fall produced two effects, one physical and one spiritual. As to the physical, our flesh became liable to disease, death, decay, and corruption. And as to the spiritual, we come into this world damned and doomed and incapable of doing any good whatever.

Now in theory, created matter and created flesh still remain good. They have not become evil, and the soul remains an image of God, even though it has lost all likeness to God through sin. As Augustine himself says,

> No one accuses the substance of our body, no one accuses the nature of the flesh. There is no point in your demonstrating the cleanliness of what we do not find blameworthy! We do not deny that there are within us evil desires, to which, if we live as we should, we should not consent. They must be punished, they must be checked, they must be vanquished, but they are ours, not someone else's. And they are not our good things, but our evil things.[25]

But it is a small step to go from saying "the flesh is not evil, but is full of evil desires and cannot do good," to "the flesh is evil." Likewise, it is a small step to go from saying "the world is not evil, but is full of things that will lure, seduce, and tempt us into evil," to "the world itself is evil." We must remember, too, that for the men and women of the twelfth century, death was all around them, and they saw everywhere with their own eyes the decay and corruption that were the result of the Fall. And what does Genesis 2:7 say? It says that the Lord God created human beings *de limo terrae*, "from the *limus* of the earth." And what does *limus* mean? It means mud, filth, mire, or slime. We are not surprised, then, to read in the *De miseria conditionis humanae* of the future Pope Innocent III, that

25. Augustine, *Contra Julianum* VI.xxiii.74; PL 44:868.

> the Lord God created human beings from the slime of the earth, which is inferior to any of the other elements. He made the planets and stars from fire, he made the breezes and winds from air, he made the fish and the birds from water, he made cattle and human beings from earth. If, then, we consider the creatures made from water, we will find ourselves to be vile. If we consider those made from air, we will know ourselves to be yet more vile. If we consider those made from fire, we will believe ourselves to be most vile. We cannot make ourselves equal to the things in the heavens, nor dare we put ourselves above the things on the earth, for we find ourselves on a par with cattle, and recognize ourselves to be just like them.[26]

And the author of the *Meditationes* says the same thing, if more briefly: "you are a human being: earthly from the earth, slime from slime. Of the earth you are, from the earth you live, and to the earth you will return when that last day comes—and it will come suddenly, perhaps today!" (§10).

This certainly puts us in our place, and the future pope goes on to examine the disgusting food of the fetus in the womb, the weakness of the infant, the pains of old age, the miserable state of masters as well as servants, the miserable state of the married as well as the celibate, and the miserable state of just about anybody. When I got to the end of the book I was ready to throw myself off the nearest cliff, which is not difficult here in Newfoundland. *Ps.-*Bernard is actually much more balanced, and although we have plenty of material from the *contemptus mundi* tradition, he never loses sight of the inherent dignity of the image of God.

But although we have retained the image, we have lost the likeness through sin, and it is time now to say something more about sin, not of its Augustinian reality, but about its categories.

---

26. Lotario dei Segni (Pope Innocent III), *De Miseria Condicionis Humanae*, ed. and trans. Robert E. Lewis, The Chaucer Library (Athens, GA: University of Georgia Press, 1978), 97.

Traditional Roman Catholic teaching distinguishes two sorts of sin, mortal and venial. The classic formulation of this, but not its first occurrence, is to be found in the work of Thomas Aquinas. A mortal sin cuts the sinner off entirely from the grace of God, and it follows logically that if a sinner dies in a state of mortal sin, the only place he or she can go is hell. In modern Roman Catholicism, it is not easy to commit mortal sin. Three conditions are required. First, it must concern a "grave matter," though what matters are considered grave has changed over the centuries. Murder, obviously, is a grave matter, as is adultery, incest, idolatry, and a variety of other offences, but it cannot be denied that there are blurred edges here. Second, it must be committed with the full and complete knowledge of the gravity of the offense. And third, it must be committed with what is technically known as advertence, the deliberate and complete consent of the will. In other words, you cannot commit mortal sin by accident, and you cannot commit mortal sin if you are not in full possession of your faculties. What must be noted here is that it is not the act itself that defines mortal sin, but the state of mind in which it is committed.

A venial sin is anything less than this. It may be extremely serious, but it does not cut one off entirely from the saving grace of God. According to Aquinas (and the modern Roman Catholic Church), if one dies in a state of unconfessed venial sin, God will forgive the guilt of that sin by an act of unconditional grace, though one will still be punished for having committed it by the cleansing flames of purgatory. To the question of purgatory we shall return in a moment.

In the twelfth century the situation was dramatically different. John McManners, speaking of the seventeenth and eighteenth centuries, says that "most sins were mortal; a venial sin would be something like speaking an idle, frivolous word, or stealing something of no consequence like an apple or a pin,"[27] and this

---

27. John McManners, *Church and Society in Eighteenth-Century France,* 2 vols. (Oxford: Clarendon Press, 1998), 2:246.

was also the case in the Middle Ages. Furthermore, as far as one can gather, most parish priests judged an act as mortally sinful or venially sinful simply by the action itself, taking little account of the motives behind it or the psychological state of the sinner. In other words, when *ps.*-Bernard or the future Pope Innocent III was writing, it was easy to commit mortal sin and easy to go to hell. The clear distinction drawn by Aquinas post-dates them, of course, though the principle that some sins are more serious than others and have graver consequences goes back to the earliest days of Christianity. It is also true that in the second half of the twelfth century, we see a movement toward emphasizing the importance of the state of mind in which a sin is committed. This is evident in the literature dealing with *conscientia* that we mentioned in the last chapter, and was particularly important for Peter Abelard, whose "intentionalist ethics" stated that the moral worth of an action was dependent on the intention of the agent.[28] The average parish priest, however, was not reading Abelard, who had already been condemned for heresy in 1141, and dealt with his penitents by what they did, not by what they thought.

Sin and sinning appear throughout the *Meditationes*, but the author makes no distinction between the various categories of sin. Sin is sin is sin. This fact inevitably leads him to emphasize the need for confession, and, as we saw in the last chapter, he leaves us in no doubt as to its importance. In this, he is following in the footsteps of a host of others, not least Bernard himself, whose fortieth sermon *de diversis*—a sermon that *ps.*-Bernard certainly knew—is dedicated to the subject. Bernard begins by saying that if you wish to follow the ways of life—he is quoting Psalm 15:11— there are two main ways: confession, which washes away sins, and obedience, which strengthens virtues. As to confession, there are seven steps: self-knowledge, penance or repentance,[29] sorrow,

28. A very great deal has been written and continues to be written on this subject, but for a clear and concise summary, see Peter King, "Abelard's Intentionalist Ethics," *The Modern Schoolman* 72 (1995): 213–23.

29. *Poenitentia* in Latin means both penance and repentance.

confession by mouth or vocal confession, mortification of the flesh, correcting what you do, and perseverance.

Every one of these appears in the *Meditationes*, though not in the same order and not as a formal list. It is not our business here to examine what Bernard has to say in detail, and those interested can read it for themselves.[30] It is well worth reading. But what is eminently clear is the vital importance of confession in the spiritual life. Confession, says Bernard,

> is good equipment for the soul. It cleanses a sinner and makes a righteous person cleaner. If there are sins, they are washed away in confession; if there are good deeds, they are commended by confession. When you confess your wicked deeds, an afflicted spirit is a sacrifice to God [Ps 50:19]. When [you confess] what good things God has done for you, you offer to God a sacrifice of praise [Ps 49:14]. Without confession, a righteous person is judged ungrateful and a sinner considered dead. Confession, therefore, is the life of the sinner and the glory of the righteous.[31]

Confession could also serve a useful psychological and sociological function. An experienced confessor could certainly provide counseling to a distraught penitent,[32] and the confessional also allowed the parish priest to know what was going on in his parish. An experienced pastor, therefore, might well be able to defuse dangerous situations and avert problems before they occurred.

There were manuals for confessors in the twelfth century, though the great burgeoning of such texts took place later, after the Fourth Lateran Council in 1215. In its twenty-first canon, the Council

---

30. There is a good English translation in *Bernard of Clairvaux: Monastic Sermons*, trans. Daniel Griggs, intro. Michael Casey, CF 68 (Collegeville, MN: Cistercian Publications, 2016), 201–12.

31. Bernard, *De diversis, sermo* 40.2; SBOp 6/1:235.

32. See Alexander Murray, *Conscience and Authority in the Medieval Church* (Oxford: Oxford University Press, 2015), chap. 3 "Counselling in Medieval Confession."

required annual confession for every adult, male and female alike, of whatever station in life.[33] And if someone should say that confession to God alone is quite sufficient (for does not forgiveness come ultimately from God?), and that confession to a priest is unnecessary, the author of the *Meditationes* has an answer:

> Confession is useless unless it is made with a truthful tongue and a pure heart. And in order for three to bear witness to us in heaven, the Father, Son, and Holy Spirit [see 1 John 5:7], let us add the witness of the priest to that of our heart and our mouth, so that "in the mouth of two or three witnesses every word shall stand." (§25; quoting Matt 18:16 and 2 Cor 13:1)

If, then we confess our sins truly, sincerely, and completely, we might, by God's grace, enter Paradise. But where else might we go? That, in a sense, is up to us. When we die and our soul appears before the Supreme Judge, what will happen? It is our deeds, our own actions, that will accuse us! "You committed us!" they will say,

> We are your deeds! We shall not leave you, but will be with you always, and will go with you to Judgment!" The vices, too, will accuse the soul with many and manifold sins, and will invent many false testimonies against it, even though those that are true can be quite sufficient for its damnation.

33. Most of the literature dealing with confession and the manuals for confessors concentrates, understandably, on the thirteenth century and later, but for our purposes, three studies are fundamental: Pierre Michaud-Quantin, *Sommes de casuistique et manuels de confession au moyen âge (XII–XVI siècles)* (Louvain: Nauwelaerts, 1962); Leonard E. Boyle, "Summa confessorum," in *Les genres littéraires dans les sources théologiques et philosophiques médiévales: Définition, critique et exploitation* (Louvain: Publications de l'Institut d'Études médiévales, 1982), 227–37; and Joseph Goering, "The Internal Forum and the Literature of Penance and Confession," in *The History of Medieval Canon Law in the Classical Period, 1140–1234: From Gratian to the Decretals of Pope Gregory IX,* ed. Wilfried Hartmann and Kenneth Pennington (Washington, DC: Catholic University of America Press, 2008), 379–428.

> Demons will terrify it with their terrible faces and horrifying
> appearance: they will pursue it with great fury and seize it,
> terribly and horribly, seeking to keep it and possess it, unless
> there be someone to rescue it. (§5)

There are no psychological niceties here, no subtleties of inten-
tionality. We will be condemned or delivered by what we do, and
that is all there is to it. But are these pains that *ps.*-Bernard describes
so vividly the pains of hell or the pains of purgatory? According
to Bernard himself, there is a region called the region of expiation
where the souls of the dead are assigned to three different locations
according to their different merits: hell, purgatory, and heaven.

> In hell are the wicked; in purgatory those who need purg-
> ing; in heaven, those who have been perfected. Those in
> hell cannot be redeemed, for in hell there is no redemption.
> Those in purgatory await redemption but are first tormented,
> either by flaming fire or bitter cold or some other terrible
> pain. Those in heaven rejoice in joy at the vision of God.
> They are Christ's brothers and sisters in nature, co-heirs in
> glory, like him in delightful eternity.[34]

But since there is nothing we can do for the first group, Bernard
continues, who do not deserve redemption, nor for the third group,
who do not need it, he will concentrate on the second group, those
in purgatory. He will beg help for them with groans and sighs, he
will intercede for them, he will hope that his own sacrifices will
be of assistance to them, for their punishment can be shortened
by kind services such as these.

The classic study of the development of purgatory was published in 1984 by the late Jacques Le Goff,[35] who dates the idea
of purgatory as a physical place with fire and flames to the period

---

34. Bernard, *De diversis, sermo* 42.5; SBOp 6/1:259.

35. Jacques Le Goff, *The Birth of Purgatory* (Chicago: University of Chicago
Press, 1984).

between about 1170 and 1200. I cannot say I agree with him, for the descriptions we find in Bernard and a number of other writers seem to me to indicate an earlier date. But whatever its history, there can be no doubt of the importance of purgatory, not least in what might be called its spin-offs, especially the sale of indulgences. This began in 1095 when Pope Urban II promised a plenary indulgence to all those who were prepared to take part in the First Crusade.

But despite its importance, and despite Bernard's speaking of it numerous times, there is no mention of purgatory in the *Meditationes*. There is no doubt in my mind that the author had read or heard Bernard's forty-second sermon *de diversis*, and he has clearly been influenced by Bernard's description of hell or Gehenna in that same sermon,[36] but the region of purging or purification makes no appearance whatever. I admit that I find this surprising, and I can offer no satisfactory reason as to why it should be so. The readers of the *Meditationes* go straight to hell or heaven. There is no third choice.

As to the descriptions of hell and heaven, sufficient has been said on that matter in chapter one. They are just as we might expect them to be and are paralleled in a multitude of other sources. The most important practical question, therefore, is clear and obvious: how do we avoid the one and deserve the other? That will be the subject of our next chapter.

36. See n. 58 to the translation.

CHAPTER FOUR

The Teaching of the *Meditationes*: Practice

The *Meditationes* are not mystical. I said that in chapter one and have no hesitation in repeating it here. It is an important point. On the other hand, they are certainly spiritual, if we follow Pelagius or one of his followers, who defined spirituality simply as holding on to what is good and making progress therein.[1] In more recent times, Geoffrey Wainwright has defined spirituality as "the combination of praying and living,"[2] though most writers eschew such down-to-earth definitions, and prefer to dwell on concepts of self-transcendence or the inner dimension where the seeker experiences ultimate reality.[3] Robert Swanson has rightly pointed out the danger of these approaches:

1. *Ps.*-Jerome, *Epistola* 7.8; PL 30:114D–15A (= PL 30:385A).

2. *The Study of Spirituality*, ed. Cheslyn Jones, Geoffrey Wainwright, and Edward Yarnold (Oxford: Oxford University Press, 1986), 9, 592.

3. For this and what follows, see David N. Bell, "Twelfth-Century Commentaries on the Song of Songs and the Nature of Monastic Spirituality: A Reassessment," in *Il Cantico dei Cantici nel Medioevo. Atti del Convegno Internazionale dell'Università degli Studi di Milano e della Società Internazionale per lo Studio del Medioevo Latino. Gargnano sul Garda, 22–24 maggio 2006*, ed. Rossana E. Guglielmetti (Florence: Sismel—Edizioni del Galluzzo, 2008), 371–96 (here 375).

> Our squeamishness, and insistence on a definition of spiri-
> tuality which tends to invalidate anything which does not
> approach the mystical—and preferably the Dionysian ver-
> sion of mysticism through the penetration of the darkness
> surrounding an ineffable divinity, rather than that which
> offered an affective, emotion-centred and emotion-directed
> access to God—places a major barrier between the twentieth
> century and pre-Reformation religious practices.[4]

According to Thomas of Perseigne, whom we met in chapter
two, people in general may be divided into three groups: the *bruti*
or *carnales*, the *activi* or *spirituales*, and the *contemplativi* or *in-
tellectuales*. In the first case, the senses and thinking are defiled.
In the second, the affections are beautified and action adorned. In
the third, the intellect is transcended and reason raised to a higher
state.[5] But those who belong to the third group are few, and the
great majority of monks and nuns were the *activi* or *spirituales*,
those concerned with setting in order their inner disposition and
acting outwardly in an appropriate way.

It must be remembered, too, that in the Middle Ages, the distinction commonly made nowadays between thought and action—
what we think and what we do—was far less clearly delineated.
As Norman Tanner has said,

> For medieval people there was far less of a distinction be-
> tween the outer and the inner aspects of religion than for us
> today. . . . Medieval people thought and expressed them-
> selves largely by what they did, and therefore their external

---

4. Robert N. Swanson, *Catholic England: Faith, Religion and Observance
Before the Reformation* (Manchester and New York: Manchester University
Press, 1993), 22; Bell, "Twelfth-Century Commentaries," 375.

5. Thomas of Perseigne, *In Cantica canticorum*, I.1; PL 206:68BC: *In primo
ordine sensus sordidatur et cogitatio; in secundo ornatur affectus et honestatur
actio; in tertio sublimatur intellectus et vegetatur ratio.* Thomas has taken this
directly from *ps.*-Julian of Toledo, *In Nahum*, 5; PL 96:712B. The Nahum commentary is also quoted by *ps.*-Bernard.

activities were the key to, indeed for the most part *were*, their inner piety.[6]

The *ps.*-Bernardine *Meditationes* were compiled precisely for the *activi* or *spirituales*. They were not a guide for the high-flying *contemplativi*, and the concern of the author was to have his readers appreciate their own sinful degradation and stimulate them to restore the lost likeness. How? By the loss of self, not the loss of self in any mystical or experiential way, but by the loss of self-will or self-love. For "the less we do our own will, the more we can do God's will; and the more we do God's will, the more we become like him."[7] The author of the *Meditationes* never uses the terms self-will or self-love—*voluntas propria* or *amor propria*—but the principle runs through the entire work. Spirituality here is exactly what Pelagius said it was: holding on to what is good and making progress therein—or, in other words, eradicating the vices and cultivating the virtues. In the *De spiritu et anima*, a text closely associated with the *Meditationes*, the unknown author puts the matter in a nutshell: we honor the divine likeness "by the excellence of our behavior, the practice of the virtues, and the worthiness of our merits."[8]

There is nothing whatever new in the practical teaching of the *Meditationes*, but what the author says is not arranged point by point as it is in the *Octo puncta perfectionis assequendae* that we glanced at in chapter one. There are themes, certainly—*contemptus mundi*, self-knowledge, and so on—but as Cédric Giraud has pointed out so clearly, the approach of the *Meditationes* is essentially meditative. By reading what *ps.*-Bernard says and

---

6. Norman Tanner, "Piety in the Later Middle Ages," in *A History of Religion in Britain: Practice and Belief from Pre-Roman Times to the Present*, ed. Sheridan Gilley and W. J. Sheils (Oxford: Blackwell, 1994), 71; Bell, "Twelfth-Century Commentaries," 389.

7. Bell, "Twelfth-Century Commentaries," 391.

8. *De spiritu et anima*, 35; PL 40:806; Bell, "Twelfth-Century Commentaries," 391–92.

pondering on it, we may come to an awareness of our own sinfulness. This is essential, for as the author says, "you cannot cure a disease that you do not know you have" (§31). This will lead to *compunctio* or compunction, a word the author uses four times. The principle goes back to the time of the Desert Fathers, and, as the Benedictine Claude Peifer has said, it is "no morbid or cowardly grief indicating weakness of character; it is the attitude of the saint who fully realizes the depths of his own misery and the reality of the evil of sin":[9]

> This profound sense of sin which is the basis for compunction is no morbid, pathological pessimism nor Freudian guilt complex, but an eminently realistic view of the fallen state of human nature and the actual fact of man's departure from God.[10]

For the oriental monks, he adds, it also included weeping over one's sins, something that later became known as the gift of tears. This is just what we find in the *Meditationes*. "Weep for your iniquities and sins by which you have offended God" (§14), says *ps.*-Bernard, and he laments that he cannot now weep for himself, for the grace of tears, the *gratia lacrymarum*, has been taken from him. The concept of the gift or grace of tears is a matter on which much has been written in recent years,[11] and in the *Meditationes*

---

9. Claude J. Peifer, *Monastic Spirituality* (New York: Sheed and Ward, 1966), 209.

10. Peifer, *Monastic Spirituality*, 212.

11. See especially Piroska Nagy, "Religious Weeping as Ritual in the Medieval West," *Social Analysis: The International Journal of Anthropology* 48 (2004): 119–37; and Diane Apostolos-Cappadona, " 'Pray with Tears and Your Request Will Find a Hearing': On the Iconology of the Magdalene's Tears," in *Holy Tears: Weeping in the Religious Imagination*, ed. Kimberley C. Patton and John S. Hawley (Princeton: Princeton University Press, 2005), 201–28, but especially 205–8, "Towards a Christian Theology of Tears." Much further information may be found in *Crying in the Middle Ages: Tears of History*, ed. Elina Gertsman (New York: Routledge, 2012).

the monk weeps not only for his own sins but for those of others as well, especially for those who are not aware that they are sinners.

This is why a daily examination of oneself—the subject of chapter five of the *Meditationes*—is so important. It is a standard monastic practice, and the daily Examen so clearly and simply set out by Ignatius of Loyola sets forth what is required. For him, there are five stages, and we see all five in the *Meditationes*, though not so clearly set out. First, we must remember that we are in the presence of God, who is everywhere present and everywhere whole. Second, we look back over the day and think of just a few things, maybe just two or three, that God has done for us and for which we are grateful. We thank him for this. Third, we review the day from start to finish, looking over what we did and whether we did it well or not. This, says *ps.*-Bernard, is when we

> take careful note of how much we advance [in virtue] and in how much we fall back, what we are like in our outward actions and what we are like in our feelings, how similar we are to God, and how dissimilar, how near to him or how far from him, not by any spatial distance, but by how we act and think. (§14)

We must be absolutely honest in this, for all of us know how easily and subtly we can deceive ourselves. The fourth stage is then sorrow—compunction—for the sins we have committed, joined with a determination to commit them no more, and a prayer to God for forgiveness. And fifth and finally, we ask for God's grace to help us control our longings, direct our actions, and amend our ways, for without grace we can do nothing, and, as Augustine said, "of our own power we can only fall."[12] Much of what *ps.*-Bernard says in his chapter on the daily examination of oneself is taken from Hugh of Saint-Victor's *De institutione novitiorum*, but the author has made it very much his own.

12. See chap. 3, n. 23.

The Chapter of Faults is intended to help us in realizing our sinfulness. No one is more skilled than we at deceiving ourselves, and we are extremely proficient at making our vices look like virtues. We may not particularly like being corrected—chapter ten, on the dislike of being corrected, is beautifully done, and the author has woven together his sources most effectively—but there is no doubt that we need it. The Chapter of Faults was a meeting of the monastic community held in the Chapter Room at which any member of the community could accuse either himself or any other member of the community of some infraction of the Rule or usages. This was referred to as the *clamatio* or *proclamatio*, and the formula used was "I proclaim Brother so-and-so . . . ." It was particularly associated with the Cistercians in the twelfth century, but it was not a Cistercian invention. It developed in the eighth and ninth centuries, and the Cluniac customary provides detailed instructions as to how it was to be conducted. Chapter 46 of the Rule of Saint Benedict makes provision for public confession of faults by individual members of the community, but not for a Chapter of Faults in which the members might accuse or proclaim each other. There is no doubt that the Chapter of Faults could be contaminated by petty jealousies and the consequences of self-love, but one can see the logic of it, even if one does not agree with it.

For medieval men and women, the recognition of their own sinfulness was a sure indication that hell loomed before them. This is something we discussed in the last chapter, and it is intimately linked to the need for confession, a matter on which we have said enough earlier. We have also pointed out that death came early in the Middle Ages, especially among the peasantry, and that death, like God, was everywhere present. In much of the modern world, though not in all parts, death has been sanitized, and dead bodies, if they are not kept hidden, are exposed to view only after they have been transformed by the skills of the mortician. I well remember the squeamishness of groups of students that at one time I was leading round France when, in French markets, they came across butchers' stalls with mounds of dead animals and birds, still with their fur and feathers, obviously very dead. They were, of course, used to seeing their meat neatly packaged in plastic and bearing no resemblance to the animal from which it came.

But when the author of the *Meditationes* looks into the tombs of those who have died, what does he find? "Nothing but ashes and worms, stench and horror," and he quotes a passage that directly anticipates the very popular legend of the Three Dead Kings or the Three Living and the Three Dead: *Quod ego sum, ipsi fuerunt; et quod ipsi sunt, ego ero*, "What I am, they have been, and what they are, I shall be" (§4). This is a precursor of a very popular epitaph that appears in slightly variant forms on countless early grave-stones: "Remember me as you walk by: As you are now, so once was I; As I am now, so you will be: Prepare yourself to follow me!"

The story of the Three Living and the Three Dead appears in a number of late medieval poems and in a host of illustrations from the thirteenth century onwards. There are many differences in detail, but the essential features remain the same. Three young noblemen are out hunting and lose their way in a wood. There they come across three unburied bodies (or in some cases, three walking corpses) in various stages of decay, all graphically described. Looking on these with horror, they are yet more horrified when one or more of the cadavers opens its mouth and croaks, "As you are now, so once were we. As we are now, so you shall be." And the young men, understandably, are never quite the same again. One of the earliest poems on the theme is the *Dit des trois morts et des trois vifs* by Baudouin de Condé, who was active between 1240 and 1280, but the line in the *Meditationes* seems to indicate that the tale itself was considerably earlier.

Meditation on death has been a standard monastic practice for centuries. In 1683, when Armand-Jean de Rancé, abbot of la Trappe, published his great work on the holiness and duties of the monastic life, he included a section on meditation on death and quoted as his authorities Cyprian of Carthage, John Chrysostom, Ephrem Syrus, Saint Benedict, John of the Ladder, and Bernard of Clairvaux. Nor was he in any doubt about the usefulness of the meditation:

> It arouses one's fervor, banishes all laziness, puts an end to
> the soul's fickleness, prevents the mind from wandering,
> makes penance pleasant, destroys the distaste for humili-
> ations, allays intemperate words, does away with all earthly
> cares, brings about strict watchfulness [over oneself], pro-
> duces pure and ardent prayer, and inspires and preserves
> devotion.[13]

Had he lived a few centuries later, the author of the *Meditationes* would have been delighted with this. Arousing fervor, banishing laziness, curbing the fickle nature of the heart, doing away with earthly cares, watching over oneself, inspiring devotion, and the importance of prayer: all these are considered in the treatise. Penance, however, is not. The Latin word *poenitentia*, which can mean both penance and repentance, appears just four times in the text, and each time the context makes it clear that the author is speaking of repentance, change of heart, turning from *transitoria* to *eternalia*, rather than penance. There is but one brief passage, borrowed from Bernard, in which the author speaks of treating the body harshly, "for if you cannot offer it up all at once for Christ, then at least offer it up by a milder if longer martyrdom."[14]

Bernard himself, the genuine Bernard, also emphasizes the importance of repentance—it is the second of the seven steps necessary for effective confession that we spoke of in the last chapter—but he also lays stress on the need for corporeal penance. In one of his sermons *de diversis*, he deals with three things necessary for penance, based on the fact that there are three states of the soul: in the body, out of the body in death, and returned to the body in the resurrection. The first state was given to the soul so that it might do penance; the second and third states involve its reward or punishment according to its merits (or lack of them) in

13. Armand-Jean de Rancé, *De la sainteté et des devoirs de la vie monastique*, 2 vols. (Paris: F. Muguet, 1683), 1:427.

14. See n. 92 to the translation.

this life. But there are also three things needful for doing penance: the time, the body, and the place.

Now time too may be divided into three[15]—past, present, and future—and penance applies to all of them. We do penance for what we have done in the past, we do good works in the present, and we always have a good intention to do better in the future, for it is those who persevere to the end who shall be saved (Matt 10:22). What, then, of the body? A body is essential if we are to do penance, for if penance were a matter for the soul (*animus*) alone, it would be unbearably burdensome. But since soul and body work together, "the more the body is burdened, the more the soul is unburdened."[16] As to the place, this is the church of this present life, "and anyone who neglects to do penance correctly while still living in the body will not be able to obtain the remedy of salvation in the future."[17] In other words, for Bernard, penance is essential, but as he says elsewhere, very sensibly, *ne quid nimis*, "do not do it to excess." Excessive fervor can easily get out of hand and do injury to unity.[18]

There is nothing of this in the *Meditationes*: only that one single mention of "a milder if longer martyrdom." *Ps.*-Bernard's concern is more with the spiritual *conversatio morum*, "change in one's way of life," mentioned in the Rule of Saint Benedict (58.17), though he does not use the actual expression. To achieve this we need all the help we can get, and there are two principal ways in which this help might be obtained. They are love and prayer, and

---

15. These threefold divisions appear everywhere in the theological and spiritual literature of the time, and can be rather tiresome. The best (or worst) example is the commentary on the Song of Songs of Thomas of Perseigne.

16. Bernard, *De diversis, sermo* 106.2; SBOp 6/1:378.

17. Bernard, *De diversis, sermo* 106.2; SBOp 6/1:378.

18. Bernard, *De diversis, sermo* 108; SBOp 6/1:382. The sermon concerns the need for bloodletting, which is a penance in itself. See generally the old but sound account by Percy Fleming, "The Medical Aspects of the Medieval Monastery in England," *Proceedings of the Royal Society of Medicine* 22 (1928): 774–75.

the author of the *Meditationes* has much to say on both. Let us begin with love.[19]

What the author has to say on the subject is scattered throughout the treatise. There is nothing systematic about his presentation, nothing like the four degrees of love of the genuine Bernard, and certainly nothing about drops of water being lost in wine or red-hot iron merging with fire, or the air, bright with light, seeming to become light itself.[20] As we saw in the last chapter, *ps.*-Bernard follows Augustine in seeing love not only as a gift of the Holy Spirit, but as the Holy Spirit itself. Nothing could be more important. We must remember that for all those Westerners who followed in the footsteps of Augustine, it was impossible to do even a single good action by our own power. All that we are is wholly dependent on God. If we exist at all, we exist only because we participate in his being. If we live, it is by participation in his life. If we sense, it is by participation in his sensing. And if we reason, it is only by participation in his rationality, who is the Supreme Reason. This is reflected in the Great Chain of Being,[21] which begins with minerals and progresses through plants, animals, humans, and angels, to God himself. The genesis of the idea lies with Plato, Aristotle, Plotinus, and Proclus, but it was taken up and elaborated by a host of medieval theologians and philosophers, whom it is not our business here to investigate.

But if we are to love God, it can only be because he loved us first,[22] and then, by his grace, we may participate in that love (which is the Holy Spirit) and love him in return. In other words, we can love God not by our own strength, not by our own power, but only by the power of the Holy Spirit whom God offers to us. It is possible to take this idea much further and say that if we par-

19. The three words for love—*amor*, *dilectio*, and *caritas*—were discussed in chap. 3.

20. Bernard, *De diligendo Deo* 10.28; SBOp 3:143.

21. The classic study is Arthur O. Lovejoy, *The Great Chain of Being: A Study of the History of an Idea* (Cambridge, MA: Harvard University Press, 1936), with many subsequent reprintings.

22. 1 John 4:19, quoted at the beginning of §2.

ticipate in love, and if love is the Holy Spirit, then if we realize or actualize our participation in the Holy Spirit, we may find ourselves experiencing a true mystical experience in the very midst of the Trinity. This is the path taken by William of Saint-Thierry, whose pneumatocentric mysticism leads to heights beyond all words and all descriptions. But this, as we have seen, is emphatically not the way of the author of the *Meditationes*.

His concern is solely with transferring our love of the world and worldly pleasures to God and divine things, from *transitoria* to *eternalia*, from dross and sin to splendor and glory and the restoration of the lost likeness. He says so again and again, for "those who love the world more than God, life in the world more than the cloister, gluttony more than abstinence, lechery more than chastity, follow the devil and go with him into eternal torment" (§35). But a love for God cannot be separated from a love for human beings, and one of the clearest presentations of this is to be found in the works of Baldwin, abbot of Forde and eventually archbishop of Canterbury, but who was not one of *ps.*-Bernard's sources. The love of God, says Baldwin, is made known and strengthened in the love of our neighbor, for

> since God has no need of any benefits himself, he has put in its place, as it were, our love for our brothers, sisters, and neighbors who do need these things, so that they might receive from us those outstanding benefits that are due to him. None, therefore, should flatter themselves that they love God, none should deceive themselves by thinking that they love God if they do not love their neighbor, [for if they do not love their neighbor] they do not love God.[23]

Ps.-Bernard is far more concise: "Love all people, and show yourself worthy to be loved by all, so that you may be a peacemaker and a child of God."[24]

23. Baldwin of Forde, *Sermo* 15.64; CCCM 99:245.
24. See n. 204 to the translation.

The whole of human good, he says, "is to know and love the Creator,"[25] and if we are with God by loving him, he himself dwells within us. How can it be otherwise? If love is both the Holy Spirit and the gift of the Holy Spirit, then if the love of God is in our hearts, the Holy Spirit is in our hearts, and since the Holy Spirit cannot be separated from the Father and the Son, it follows that when "the love [*caritas*] of God is poured forth in our hearts [Rom 5:5], the whole Trinity dwells within us" (§3, last lines).

The more we love God, says *ps.*-Bernard, the more closely shall we see him (§37, last line), but the fullness of love and the full vision of God are reserved for the next life (see §12). *Ps.*-Bernard, as we have said earlier, has much to say on the joys and delights of Paradise, and it is his heartfelt prayer that, by God's grace, he may so overcome the old self, the *vetus homo*, that he may be found worthy to be admitted into the kingdom of God to enjoy them.[26]

Prayer is of vital importance to *ps.*-Bernard, and what he has to say of it is presented more systematically than almost anything else in the text. Three whole chapters of the *Meditationes*—chapters six to eight—are devoted to prayer and praying, and the author has selected his sources from half a dozen different writers. The most important are Bernard and Augustine, but he also includes Jerome, Gregory the Great, Lawrence of Novara,[27] and Seneca the Younger.

What *ps.*-Bernard has to say about prayer can be summarized in five points. The first is the need to quieten the mind and focus our will and intention on God. There's no use being silent outwardly if we're prattling away inwardly. This is standard teaching on prayer and finds its culmination in the hesychast tradition in the Orthodox East. This is by no means easy, for as the author says, there is nothing more fickle than the human heart, and keeping control of our thoughts is extraordinarily difficult. But if we pray

25. See n. 116 of the translation.
26. See the whole of the last chapter of the *Meditationes*, §§38–40.
27. See chap. 2, nn. 36–39.

just with our mouth and our mind wandering far away, our prayer will avail us nothing. Putting it another way, prayer with the mouth without the intention of the heart and mind is useless.

The second point is the need to listen. Pay heed to God, he says, who pays heed to you:

> Listen to him speaking to you so that he might listen to you speaking to him. This will be so if, when divine praises are to be offered up, you are attentive to what you are doing with all due reverence and care, while paying careful heed to each and every word of divine Scripture. (§16)

This reminds me of Armand-Jean de Rancé's pithy dictum: prayer is as much listening as asking.[28]

The third point is that prayer can be done anywhere, for we are living temples of God, and the inward aspect of prayer is more important than the outward. We saw in chapter three how *ps.*-Bernard adapts the homily on the Canaanite woman attributed to Lawrence of Novara: you can pray anywhere, in the marketplace, in the bath, in bed, anywhere at all. "Don't look for a place, because you yourself are the place! Just pray, and there's your temple!" (§17).

The fourth point is that we should pray often, continually even, though the author does not specifically mention Saint Paul's injunction in 1 Thessalonians 5:17 to "pray without ceasing." He does, however, imply it, for he tells us that we should always have God before our eyes, that we should always be subject to him and attentive to him, and that he is present to us in everything we do (§§19–20). We should reckon all the time we are not thinking about God as loss, so wherever we may be, let us "cast up our thoughts to God."[29] Every time we do a good action, or try to do

28. For those interested in prayer and praying, what Rancé has to say on the subject is clear, sensible, and useful: see David N. Bell, " 'A Holy Familiarity': Prayer and Praying According to Armand-Jean de Rancé," *Cistercian Studies Quarterly* 51 (2016): 343–72.

29. See n. 182 of the translation.

a good action, that in itself is a prayer, and a life lived with God in mind is a life of ceaseless prayer. It is "the combination of praying and living" by which Geoffrey Wainwright defined spirituality.[30]

The fifth and last point is eminently sensible: if you don't get what you pray for, or if you feel that no one is listening to you, don't undervalue prayer! His source here is Bernard's fifth sermon for Lent, and Bernard tells us that since God does not undervalue prayer, neither should we undervalue it. There are only two alternatives: either God will give us what we ask, or he knows what will be more profitable for us (§18). So pray as much as you can and trust in God. He knows what he's doing.

The Rule of Saint Benedict does not say a great deal about prayer, though we must always remember that the Divine Office, about which the Rule says a very great deal, is itself a form of prayer. As Reverend Mother Bernard Payne, abbess of the Cistercian abbey of Holy Cross at Stapehill, Dorset, from 1941 to 1956, said many years ago, "Not private but liturgical prayer is the chief occupation of the Cistercian contemplative,"[31] for

> during those hours when she is engaged in the "Work of God", the choral Office, the religious is not praying as a mere individual; she is praying in and with the entire Mystical Body of Christ, both those members of it who are still on earth, and those already in eternity, and the entire Mystical Body is praying in and through her.[32]

Chapter twenty of the Rule does, however, deal with reverence (*reverentia*) in prayer. Complete humility and pure devotion are essential, and "we must know that it is not in a multitude of words that we shall be heard, but in purity of heart and the tears of com-

---

30. See n. 2 above.

31. *La Trappe in England: Chronicles of an Unknown Monastery*, by A Religious of Holy Cross Abbey, Stapehill, Dorset [Mother Bernard Payne] (London: Burns, Oates & Washbourne, 1937), 186.

32. *La Trappe in England*, 188.

punction" (RSB 20.1).[33] Prayer, therefore, should be short and pure, unless it should be prolonged by some inspiration of divine grace, but prayer in community should always be very short.

But the amount of space devoted to prayer in the Rule, says Claude Peifer, is not a sufficient indication of its importance for Benedict or his monks:

> The distinctions which are made in modern times between common and private prayer, and between vocal and mental prayer, were entirely unknown to him. For St. Benedict, as for the entire preceding tradition, these types of prayer were not to be separated and opposed to one another, but united in a single movement of the soul toward God.[34]

Such is the view of the writer of the *Meditationes*, as it is also the view of the writers whom he selected as his sources. Living the monastic life with one's eyes continually on God is no more and no less than prayer-in-action, and if *ps.*-Bernard laments that he does not and cannot always achieve this, he certainly intends to try. Here too is where prayer is so important. We can do nothing without God's help, so let us not be afraid to ask for that help. If Saint Matthew is correct, God knows what we need (which is not necessarily what we want) before we ask him (Matt 6:8), but in my own view, he still likes to be asked.

I freely admit that in the course of translating the *Meditationes*, my own view of the little treatise changed entirely. Before I began the translation, I dismissed the work as an overly pessimistic diatribe against human sin and corruption. That was a mistake, and the result of a casual glance at the more unpleasant sections of the text rather than a careful reading. It was only when I was part way through the translation that I came to realize why the work was the most popular of any work attributed to Bernard of Clairvaux,

33. We have spoken of the tears of compunction earlier in this chapter.
34. Peifer, *Monastic Spirituality*, 389.

and why it enjoyed such a vast distribution in manuscript and print and appealed to such a wide audience.

The work is not just a collection of miscellaneous sources lumped together, but a skillfully constructed compilation of carefully selected materials seamlessly woven together to form an effective treatise. Its purpose, as Cédric Giraud has so clearly shown, is to present its readers with a meditation that will lead them to amend their lives, to turn from the vain pursuit of transitory worldly pleasures, and to know and love God, which, as *ps.*-Bernard says, is the highest good of humankind. Despite its more lurid passages, the author never loses sight of the majesty of the image of God, and his grim descriptions of sin, death, and hell are designed to arouse in us a desire to restore the lost likeness. *Ps.*-Bernard, in fact, would have agreed with William of Saint-Thierry that "For this alone were we created and do we live: that we might be like God, for we were created to his image."[35]

The *Meditationes* were the first of all the works by or attributed to Bernard to be translated into English, and a number of further translations followed. My own translation presented here, therefore, is certainly not the first, though it is the first in more than three hundred years, and we need to look at these earlier versions to see why, in my view, this most recent one is necessary. That will be the subject of the next chapter.

35. William of Saint-Thierry, *Epistola ad fratres de Monte-Dei*, 259; CCCM 88:281: *Propter hoc enim solum et creati sumus et uiuimus, ut Deo similes simus. Ad imaginem enim Dei creati sumus.*

CHAPTER FIVE

The English Translations

In 1995 I had the pleasure of making a small contribution to a *Festschrift* honoring that most learned of scholars of spirituality and monasticism, Dom Jean Leclercq. It was a brief history of the English translation of works by and attributed to Bernard of Clairvaux from 1496 to 1970,[1] and I pointed out there that the earliest translations were not of Bernard himself, but of pseudo-Bernard, and that that tradition was hardly to change for more than three hundred years.[2]

There are manuscript versions of English translations of the *Meditationes*, the *Epistola de perfectione vitae*, the *Liber de modo bene vivendi*, possibly by Thomas of Froidmont, the *Speculum peccatoris*, and the popular *Epistola de cura et modo rei familiari sutilius gubernandae*, commonly attributed to Bernardus Silvestris. All circulated under the name of Bernard, but none was actually written by him.

The remarkable popularity of the *Meditationes* is reflected in the number of English translations. There are no fewer than nine of

---

1. David N. Bell, " 'In Their Mother Tongue': A Brief History of the English Translation of Works by and Attributed to Saint Bernard of Clairvaux: 1496–1970," in *The Joy of Learning and the Love of God: Studies in Honor of Jean Leclercq*, ed. E. Rozanne Elder, CS 160 (Kalamazoo/Spencer: Cistercian Publications, 1995), 291–308.
2. Bell, " 'In Their Mother Tongue,' " 291.

these,[3] some incomplete, being merely excerpts, some complete, and some, indeed, more than complete, inasmuch as the translator has had no hesitation in adding passages either to clarify the text or to accommodate it to his own Protestant sensibilities. There was only one Roman Catholic translator, the Benedictine monk Antony Batt, who died in 1651. We shall meet him in a moment.

The earliest of the complete translations to be published in England[4] was also the earliest English translation of any work by or attributed to Bernard of Clairvaux. This reflects the high esteem in which the *Meditationes* were held, and the volume appeared in 1496. It was entitled *Medytac[i]ons of saynte Bernarde*,[5] and the colophon at the end reads thus:

> Here we make an ende of this right proffytable treatys: the Meditacyons of saynt Bernarde, whyche for very favour & charytable love of all suche persones as have not understondyng in latyn: hath be[en] translated fro laten in to englissh by a devoute Student of the universytee of Cambrydge. And hath put it to be enprynted at Westme[n]stre: by Wynkyn the Worth the ix. daye of Marche: the yere of lorde .M.CCCC. lxxxxvi.

In his brief but interesting preface to the translation, the author says that he gave a properly corrected copy to the printer on September 12, 1495, and he makes it clear that a pirated edition or editions were already in circulation.[6] None of these appears to have survived, but the author provides details as to how these pirated editions could be distinguished from his own. Who the "devoute Student" was we do not know, and nowhere in the book is there any clue as to his identity. Two further editions followed,

---

3. See Bell, "Bibliography," 127.

4. There were earlier Middle English translations that survive in manuscript: see Bell, " 'In Their Mother Tongue,' " 291–92 and 301, n. 4.

5. For the long full title, see Bell, "Bibliography," 90.

6. See Bell, "Bibliography," 90–91.

both printed by Wynkyn de Worde. The first dates from about 1499, but the exact year is uncertain since the colophon is simply taken directly from the edition of 1496. A third edition was published in 1525.[7]

For the next complete translation, we must wait for more than a century. In 1611,[8] when James I was on the throne of a united England and Scotland, a certain "W.P.," a Master of Arts of the University of Cambridge, published *Saint Bernard, His Meditations: or, Sighes, Sobbes, and Teares, upon our Saviour's passion. Also his Motives to Mortification, with other Meditations.*[9] Who "W.P." was I do not know, save that he was (as he himself tells us) an M.A. of Cambridge University and undoubtedly a clergyman of the Church of England. He dedicated his book to "The Right Worshipfull, M^r. Iohn Bullocke, of the Inner Temple, Esquire," who was presumably the John Bullock, Barrister at Law of the Inner Temple, whose family seat was at Darley Abbey in Derbyshire. He was born about 1578—the exact year is unknown—and died in May 1641. He was buried at Norton in Derbyshire.[10] As the author says in his dedicatory letter, he had originally intended to dedicate his translation to John Bullock's father, but he had died before the book was ready for publication. Thus, he writes,

> I could find none more neere and deare unto me than your self, who might vouchsafe to give the first kinde entertainement to my well-intended labours, when they should come forth into the light.[11]

The book was published in two parts, and contains a great deal more than the author's somewhat expanded version of the

---

7. For bibliographical details, see Bell, "Bibliography," 90.

8. The first edition may actually have been published in 1608, but no example has ever been found: see Bell, "Bibliography," 94.

9. Bell, "Bibliography," 94.

10. See https://www.wikitree.com/wiki/Bullock-2327.

11. The second page of the unpaginated *Epistle Dedicatorie.*

Meditationes. As he himself says, he intended "to translate these divine and comfortable Meditations on the Lords Passion, and Motives to Mortification; (selected out of the workes of S. *Bernard*, and other ancient Writers, not verbally turned into English, but augmented with such other Meditations, as it pleased God to infuse into my minde)."[12] In the second part, we find his translation of the *Meditationes* and also a much expanded version of the *ps.*-Bernardine *Sermo de vita et passio Domini*. The book proved to be popular and went into four editions, the latest being published in 1631.[13]

The translation, as we have said, is sometimes adapted to suit the theology of the translator, and in the *Sighes, Sobbes, and Teares* there is a good example in the author's rendering of one of the sections dealing with confession. If not exactly banned by the Church of England in the seventeenth century, auricular confession was certainly not encouraged, and the more evangelical clergy would have nothing to do with it at all. Here, first, is what *ps.*-Bernard actually says, or, more accurately, here is what Hugh of Saint-Victor says, from whom *ps.*-Bernard has taken the passage:

> But should it so happen that a sinner is truly penitent, but that some unforeseen need arises that prevents him from coming to confession, we should firmly believe that the great High Priest fulfills in him what a mortal [priest] could not do. In this case, what this person wished to do but was not able to accomplish is considered by God as having been done, since he did not reject confession because he scorned it, but was prevented from going by [unavoidable] necessity.[14]

Here, for comparison, is the anonymous version printed by Wynkyn de Worde in 1496:

> And yf it be so that peraventure the synner be penitent, & in the artycle of nede maye not have confession: we ought to

12. The first and second pages of the unpaginated *Epistle Dedicarorie*.
13. See Bell, "Bibliography," 94.
14. The passage is to be found at the very end of §26.

byleve faythfully that the hyghe preest fulfyllyth in hym that
the mortall myght not. And in this caas it is doon & fulfyllyd
without doubte anenst god that the man truely wolde have
fulfylled but he myghte not. For contempte or dispisynge[15]
letted not his confession: but necessitee.[16]

Here now is W.P.'s rendering:

But if a sinner does truly repent, and yet by some acci-
dentall necessity be prevented that hee cannot make any
acknowledgement to such men as he hath offended, we must
confidently believe, that whatsoever is defective in him concerning such acknowledgement, is fulfilled by *Christ*, who
hath made a full satisfaction. For GOD accepteth that as
done, which a man hath beene willing, although not able
to performe.[17]

The next writer to produce a complete translation would have
had no such qualms, given that he was a Roman Catholic monk of
the Order of Saint Benedict. Antony Batt was born at an unknown
date in England, possibly in the west country, but since this was
a time when Roman Catholicism was forbidden in England—the
Forty Martyrs of England and Wales, canonized as a group by
Pope Paul VI in 1970, were all executed between 1535 and 1679—
Batt moved to the continent, where he spent the rest of his life.
When he moved is unknown, and the first certain date we have
for him is 1616, when he made his profession at the Benedictine
house of Saint Laurence in Dieulouard in northeastern France.
The church still stands. The community had been founded in 1608
when a group of exiled English Benedictines came to the town and
were given the dilapidated church of Saint Laurence for their use.
Batt spent most of his life at Dieulouard, though from about
1640 to 1642 he was with the English Benedictines at their abbey

15. I.e. Despising.
16. *Medytac[i]ons of saynte* Bernarde, [23–24] (the pages are unnumbered).
17. *Saint Bernard, His Meditations*, 79–80.

of Saint Edmund in Paris, and then at the English priory of La Celle-en-Brie, near Meaux, where he was superior and novice master. After that he probably returned to Dieulouard for his final years and died on January 12, 1651.[18] He was the author of a number of books, mostly translations of standard spiritual authorities, and the one with which we are here concerned is *A Hive of Sacred Honie-Combes Containing Most Sweet and Heavenly Counsel: Taken Out of the Workes of the Mellifluous Doctor S. Bernard, Abbot of Clareval.*[19] It is a very long book—more than six hundred pages—and contains translations of eighteen works by or attributed to Bernard, including the *Declamationes de colloquio Simonis cum Jesu* of Geoffrey of Auxerre, the *Letter to the Brethren of Mont-Dieu* and *De contemplando Deo* of William of Saint-Thierry, the *Scala claustralium* of Guigo II of La Chartreuse, and the *Speculum monachorum* of Arnulf of Bohéries. There are only two authentic works by Bernard, the *De diligendo Deo* and a number of *Parabolae*; all the other are pseudonymous.[20] The translation of the *Meditationes* appears first, on pages 1 to 56.

In his dedicatory letter, dated February 13, 1631, Batt offers his collection "To the Most High and Mightie Princesse, Marie-Henriette de Bourbon, Queen of Great Britaine, France, and Ireland, and of the Isles of the Brittish Ocean," that is to say, Queen Henrietta Maria (1609–1669), the Catholic wife of Charles I. Batt likens Queen Henrietta Maria to Queen Esther in the book of Esther, who foiled the attempts of Haman to have all the Jews in the kingdom of her husband, Ahasuerus, killed. Esther thwarts the plan and turns the tables on Haman (who is hanged on a gallows fifty cubits high), and it is the enemies of the Jews who are then slaughtered. Batt begs Henrietta Maria to imitate Esther and persuade Charles/Ahasuerus

18. See Dominic A. Bellenger, "Batt, Antony (d. 1651)," in the *Oxford Dictionary of National Biography* (online edition; 2004).

19. Bell, "Bibliography," 97–98.

20. For a detailed listing of the contents, see Bell, "Bibliography," 97.

to reconcile his favour & mercie to your poore afflicted subjects the Catholiques of England: not to have power and
leave to defend themselves against their enemies, but to
be freed and secured from vexation in their faith, the onely
thing in which they are thought wanting, by those who are
of an other beleefe.[21]

Batt's translations are remarkably sound, though he too has
his own agenda. We saw above how the Protestant W.P. translated what *ps.*-Bernard/Hugh of Saint-Victor had to say about
confession. This is how it appears in the Roman Catholic Batt's
translation:

But if perchance a sinner be truly penitent for his sinnes, but
yet at the hower of death wanteth meanes to go to confession: we ought confidently to beleeve, that the supreame
Preist doth accomplish that, which mortal could not. More-
over it is a thing evident to God, that the man truly desired,
but wanted meanes to accomplish that which was commaun-
ded: because it was not contempt that excluded confession,
but necessitie rendered the same.[22]

We see here how Batt has amended the text of the *Meditationes* to make it more restrictive. *Ps.*-Bernard simply says that if a
truly penitent person wishes to go to confession but is prevented
from doing so by some undefined and unavoidable necessity, then
God, who knows the secrets of the heart, will take care of it. Batt
restricts it to the hour of death. On the whole, however, Batt offers
us a good translation of the *Meditationes*, but it is not as good as
that provided by a certain R. Warren, M.A., and published in 1700.
Unlike the fat tome of Batt, this is a tiny book—just about five
inches by two—and is exceedingly rare. The title is *S. Bernard's
Pious Meditations. Written Originally in the Latin Tongue, and*

21. Batt, *A Hive of Sacred Honie-Combes*, *3ᵛ.
22. Batt, *A Hive of Sacred Honie-Combes*, 39.

now Translated into English, for the Use and Benefit of all serious Christians. By R. WARREN, M.A.[23]

The frontispiece depicts Mr. Warren in his bands and clerical dress, clerical hat on his head, reading a book. Under the illustration we read "Ponder my words, O Lord. Consider my meditation," which is that version of Psalm 5:1 that appears in the 1662 Book of Common Prayer. In other words, we can be sure that Mr. Warren was a clergyman of the Church of England, but I have not been able to identify him further

He dedicates his little book "To the Much Honoured and Truly Pious M[rs] Dorothy Twells, Sister to the Right Honourable and Truly Eminent Sir Nathan Wright, Lord Keeper of the Great-Seal of England,"[24] but there is no dedicatory letter. Instead, there is an interesting and quite charming letter "To the Reader," in which Mr. Warren explains why he has written the book and also introduces the question of Bernardine or *ps.*-Bernardine authorship.

There are many pious books scattered throughout the world, he says, and some may say that there is no need for any more:

> To them that may make use of this Objection, I desire to
> return this Modest Answer. Although there are very good
> Books now Extant, and a great many too, yet I may safely
> say, none so Compendious, so Devout, and of so small a
> Price, and of the same Nature as this most Religious Manual,
> which is imputed to that Incomparably Zealous Father, and
> Happy Ascetic, St. Bernard, all whose Writings are of very
> great Worth and Estimation amongst the Learned. Whether
> or no these Meditations are St. Bernard's, I do not presume
> to determine, neither do I think it proper to entertain the
> Reader with any Dispute concerning them, because it is
> wholly unnecessary. For indeed I cannot conceive of what
> Consequence or Advantage it is to any Reader to know the

23. Bell, "Bibliography," 100.

24. On Sir Nathan Wright, see Robert J. Frankle, "Wright, Sir Nathan (1654–1721)," in the *Oxford Dictionary of National Biography* (online edition; 2004).

Author of any Book, so long as his Writings are truly Orthodox, and discreetly Composed. Thus much I may venture
to add, without making an Apology for it, that there is not
only the very height of Devotion in this little Book, but even
pretty Turns of Wit and Fancy. In short therefore it does not
only beg your Candid Acceptance of it, but even your constant and diligent perusal. For it will never be troublesome to
you, neither at home not abroad, in your Parlour, nor Closet,
but will be a fit companion for you at all times, and in all
places. The oftener you Read it, the better you will Like it.[25]

There you have it. A little book written or not written—it matters not—by Saint Bernard, that happy ascetic, with pretty turns
of wit and fancy, and cheap at the price! What could be better?
Mr. Warren's translation is more accurate than any that preceded
it, as may be seen from his rendering of the section on confession
we have introduced above. Here is how he translates it:

But if perchance a Sinner is truly Penitent, and yet through
some sudden necessity cannot come to Confession, we ought
firmly to believe, that the *Supream Priest* fulfills that in
him, which a *Mortal Priest* could not do. And so now that
is look'd on as performed with *God*, which a Man would
truly have done, but could not accomplish; because 'twas
not contempt that rejected the Confession, but unavoidable
necessity, that hindered it.[26]

There are some passages, however, where Mr. Warren translated
what *ps.*-Bernard says but feels it necessary to caution his readers
that they should not take what he says too literally. Thus, when
ps.-Bernard, following Gregory the Great, says that when death
is at hand, the sinner will not only be afraid of the consequences
of sins he knows he committed, but will be even more afraid of

---

25. Pages 2–4 of the unpaginated letter "To the Reader."
26. Warren, *S. Bernard's Pious Meditations*, 91.

the consequences of sins he did not know he committed,[27] Mr. Warren adds a note:

> But we are firmly to believe and surely to Hope, that where the case of the Soul is so well, the Grace of God will overcome these Fears, and beam forth in Rays of comfort unto her.[28]

Similarly, when we find *ps.*-Bernard saying that whoever loves life in the world more than life in the cloister is following the devil and will go with him into eternal torment, Mr. Warren bids us take this with a grain of salt and is gently critical of the happy ascetic. Saint Bernard, he says,

> was an exceedingly good Man, in a Bad and Evil Age, so he set too much on the Pharisaical Mode of outward Abstinence, which is often used to good purpose, but many times to hide evil Designs; wherefore this Passage must be taken, *cum grano salis* for *Bernardus ipse non vidit omnia* ["Bernard himself does not see everything"].[29]

A year after Warren's translation another version—it cannot really be called a translation—of the *Meditationes* appeared. This was composed by the Reverend Doctor George Stanhope, a well-known and highly respected member of the Church of England who rose to be dean of Canterbury and royal chaplain. He was born to a clerical family on March 5, 1660, at Hartshorne in Derbyshire, and educated at Eton and King's College, Cambridge. He entered Holy Orders in 1685 and served in a number of benefices before being awarded the degree of Doctor of Divinity in 1697 and being ap-

---

27. The passage appears at the very end of §6.

28. Warren, *S. Bernard's Pious Meditations*, 23.

29. Warren, *S. Bernard's Pious Meditations*, 36. "Bernard himself does not see everything" was a widely circulated proverbial saying that dates back at least to the time of Chaucer. It appears at the beginning of his *Legend of Good Women*: see John S. P. Tatlock, "Chaucer's 'Bernard the Monk,'" *Modern Language Notes* 46 (1931): 21–23.

pointed chaplain to Their Royal Highnesses William III and Mary II. In 1702 he became vicar of Saint Nicholas, Deptford, in Kent, and on March 23, 1704, was appointed dean of Canterbury. When King William died in 1702, he was succeeded by Anne, who ruled as queen of England, Scotland, and Ireland from March 8, 1702, to May 1, 1707, and then, after the Acts of Union, as queen of Great Britain and Ireland until her death in 1714. She reappointed Dr. Stanhope as royal chaplain in 1702, and he outlived her by more than a dozen years, dying at Bath on March 18, 1728.[30]

The book with which we are here concerned is his *Pious Breathings. Being the Meditations of St Augustine, His Treatise of the Love of God, Soliloquies, and Manual. To which are added Select Contemplations from St Anselm and St Bernard.*[31] It was first published in 1701 and proved astonishingly popular, with no fewer than ten later editions. It was dedicated "To Her Royal Highness the Princess Anne of Denmark," which was the title by which Queen Anne was known between her marriage to Prince George of Denmark in 1683 and her accession to the throne in 1702.

Dr. Stanhope's version of the *ps.*-Bernardine text occupies pages 355 to 414 of *Pious Breathings*, but as I mentioned above, it can hardly be termed a translation, though there is translation to be found within it. It is, for the most part, a long, meditative paraphrase of the *Meditationes* with some material omitted and much more added, and *ps.*-Bernard is hardly more than a vehicle for Stanhope's High Church ideas. The passage dealing with confession that we have discussed above makes no appearance at all, and Stanhope simply substitutes his own views on the matter. So since we cannot use this passage to illustrate the Dean's style, let us turn to the very beginning of the *Meditationes*. Here are the first three pithy sentences, in which the author is primarily dependent on Saint Augustine:

30. See Rebecca L. Warner, "Stanhope, George (1660–1728)," in the *Oxford Dictionary of National Biography* (online edition; 2004).

31. Bell, "Bibliography," 100–101.

> Many there are who know many things, and do not know
> themselves. They examine others, and ignore themselves.
> They search for God in outward things, but ignore those
> inward things within which is God.

Here now is Dr. Stanhope's rendering:

> Many are deeply learned in variety of Arts and Sciences, and
> all the while continue as profoundly ignorant of themselves:
> They are inquisitive about the Affairs of other Men, and
> perfectly void of thought or care for their own. Nay, even in
> their most useful and necessary Studies, where God is the
> Subject of the Enquiry, they think to find him in the things
> without them, and overlook the evidence for him in their
> own Breasts: None of which, though within them, is yet so
> intimate and close to them, as God.[32]

This adapted version is the last of the complete, or, in Dr. Stanhope's case, more than complete, translations of the *Meditationes*.
In 1951, Horatio Grimley included a dozen or so pages of excerpts
from the *Meditationes* in his *Saint Bernard, Abbot of Clairvaux.
Selections from his Letters, Meditations, Sermons, Hymns, and
Other Writings*,[33] and more than four decades later, in 1956, Geoffrey Webb and Adrian Walker included twenty-three pages of
abridged and poorly translated selections in their *The School of
Self-Knowledge. A Symposium from Medaieval Sources*.[34] They
were not the first to publish selections from the work. That was
done in 1614 when a certain "R. B. Gent[leman]" published *The
young mans gleanings. Gathered out of Diverse Most Zealous and
Devout Fathers, and now published for the benefit of everie Christian Man, which wisheth good successe to his soule at the later*

32. Stanhope, *Pious Breathings*, 355.
33. Published by Cambridge University Press. See Bell, "Bibliography," 113.
34. Published in London by A. R. Mowbray and in New York by Morehouse-
Gorham. See Bell, "Bibliography," 121.

day,[35] which contains translations of chapters two and fifteen of the work. But so far as I am aware, after 1956 there was no other English translation of any significant part of the *Meditationes*, much less a complete translation, and it was only in 2018 that attention was once again given to *ps*.-Bernard with the publication by Cistercian Publications of a translation of three *ps*.-Bernardine works (not including the *Meditationes*).[36] This slender volume, which we mentioned in chapter one, contains an excellent introduction by Dom Elias Dietz of Gethsemani Abbey, who observes, rightly, that "it seems that the time has come to retrieve some of the 'pious and useful' material that falls under the umbrella of Pseudepigraphical works."[37]

But given that we already have several complete English translations of the *Meditationes piisimae*, what need is there for another? There are, in fact, three reasons. First, the last (and best) complete translation—that by the Reverend R. Warren—was published in 1700, and the nature of the English language, both written and spoken, has changed much since that time. Second, all the translations have flaws, and most of the translators have some sort of hidden agenda. And third, and perhaps most important, not one of the translators makes any attempt to identify *ps*.-Bernard's sources. They usually provide a limited number of scriptural references, but that is all. In fact, the first serious attempt to examine the sources did not appear until 1964 and 1965 with the research of Robert Bultot,[38] but although his work is certainly valuable, it is also limited. Cédric Giraud added a few further identifications

35. Bell, "Bibliography," 96.

36. *Three Pseudo-Bernardine Works*, trans./annot. Catena Scholarum, intro. Dom Elias Dietz, CS 273 (Collegeville, MN: Cistercian Publications, 2018). The three works are the *Formula honestae vitae*, the *Instructio sacerdotalis*, and the *Tractatus de statu virtutum humilitatis, obedientiae, timoris, et charitatis*.

37. *Three Pseudo-Bernardine Works*, 4.

38. See Bultot, "Les 'Meditationes,' " in the List of Abbreviations, and, as a sort of Appendix to that paper, Robert Bultot, "Encore les 'Méditations' Pseudo-Bernardines," *Sacris Erudiri* 16 (1965): 425–27.

in 2016,[39] but many more remained to be discovered. The result of the combined research of Bultot, Giraud, and me will be found in chapter two and in the detailed *Index of Patristic and Medieval Sources* at the end of this volume.

Here, then, is an annotated translation of this most popular of all *ps.*-Bernardine works. It is translated from the edition of Jean Mabillon, which is now freely available on the World Wide Web, but where references need to be given, I have given them from the text in volume 184 of the Patrologia Latina of the invaluable Migne. I have also used Migne to identify the many other sources used by the author of the *Meditationes*. The reason for this is simple. If the text is not different from a more modern critical edition, there is no reason why we should not use Migne, given the fact that all the volumes are freely available on the Internet. If a modern edition is demonstrably more accurate, I have, naturally, cited that, though modern editions can be extremely expensive and generally require access to a good university library. The only major exemption to this principle are the works of Saint Bernard, which are identified by means of the critical edition of the Sancti Bernardi Opera, edited by Jean Leclercq, C. Hugh Talbot, and Henri M. Rochais, and published in eight volumes between 1957 and 1977.

39. See Giraud, *Spiritualité*, 163–70. Giraud also adds many parallels between the *Meditationes, De interiori domo, Manuale,* and *De spiritu et anima.*

PART TWO

The Translation

Most Devout Meditations
On the Knowledge of
the Human Condition[1]

---

1. On the title, see chap. 2 of part one. The actual term *meditatio* never appears in the *Meditationes*, and the participle appears only twice: once as *meditantibus* in §16 and once as *meditandum* in §18.

CHAPTER ONE

On Human Dignity

1. Many there are who know many things and do not know themselves.[2] They examine others and ignore themselves. They search for God in outward things but ignore those inward things within which is God.[3] Let me return, therefore, from what is outward to what is inward, and let me rise from what is lower to what is higher,[4] so that I might know whence I come and whither I go,[5] what I am and whence I am, and thus, through [achieving] the knowledge of myself, I may be able to come to the knowledge of God. For the more I progress in the knowledge of myself, the closer I come to the knowledge of God.

In my inner self, I find in my mind three ways in which I reflect on God, perceive him, and desire him. These three are memory, understanding, and will or love.[6] By memory, I remember; by understanding, I observe; by will, I cherish. When I am mindful

2. See Bultot, "Les 'Meditationes,' " 259, who cites a passage from Peter Damian and observes that "there is no doubt that [the expression] has a long history."

3. This sentence is a direct quotation from Augustine, *De Trinitate*, VIII. vii.11; PL 42:956.

4. This first part of the sentence is taken directly from Augustine, *Enarratio in Ps.* 145.5; PL 37:1887.

5. John 8:14.

6. *Memoria, intelligentia, voluntas/amor*: this is fully discussed in chap. 3 of part one.

of God, I find him in my memory, and in that, through him and in him, I find delight, to the extent that he himself condescends to give it to me. By understanding, I consider what God is in himself, what he is in the angels, what he is in the saints, what he is in created things, and what he is in human beings.

In himself, he is beyond comprehension, for he is the beginning and the end:[7] the beginning without beginning and the end without end. I understand from myself that God is beyond comprehension, for I cannot understand myself, whom he himself made! In the angels, he is a source of desire,[8] for they desire to look upon him. In the saints, he is a source of delight, for in him they rejoice in continual happiness. In created things, he is a source of wonder, for he creates all things powerfully, governs them wisely, and manages them benignly.[9] In human beings he is a source of love, for he is their God, and they are his people.[10] In them he dwells as in his temple, and they are his temple.[11] He scorns neither one person nor the whole people. Whoever is mindful of him understands and loves him when he is with them.

2. We should love him because he loved us first[12] and made us to[13] his image and likeness,[14] something he wished to bestow on no other creature. We are made to the image of God, that is, to the understanding and knowledge of the Son, through whom we understand and know the Father, and are able to approach him.[15]

7. Rev 22:13.

8. The section from "By understanding, I consider what God is in himself" to here is echoing Bernard, *De diversis, sermo* 48; SBOp 6/1:268.

9. This sentence appears almost word for word in *De spiritu et anima*, 52; PL 40:818.

10. See Exod 6:7; Jer 24:7; 2 Cor 6:16; Heb 8:10, and numerous other places.

11. See 1 Cor 3:16; 2 Cor 6:16.

12. 1 John 4:19.

13. The significance of *ad* rather than *in*, in *ad imaginem et similitudinem suam* is discussed in chap. 3 of part one.

14. Gen 1:26.

15. Eph 2:18: *per ipsum habemus accessum.*

Such knowledge exists between us and the Son of God because he is himself the image of God and we are made to his image.[16] But the likeness itself also testifies to this knowledge, for we are made not only to his image, but also to his likeness. It is only appropriate, then, that what is [made] to the image should reflect the image, and not merely share the name *image* to no purpose.[17] Let us, therefore, show forth his image in ourselves in a desire for peace, a regard for truth, and a love of charity.[18] Let us hold him in our memory, carry him in our conscience,[19] and worship him who is present everywhere.[20]

Our mind[21] itself, in fact, is his image, insofar as it has the capacity [to receive] him and is able to participate in him.[22] It follows, then, that the mind is not his image because it remembers

16. See further David N. Bell, *The Image and Likeness: The Augustinian Spirituality of William of Saint-Thierry*, CS 78 (Kalamazoo, MI: Cistercian Publications, 1984), 52–54.

17. From "Such knowledge" to this point is dependent on Bernard, *In Cantica, sermo* 80.i.2; SBOp 2:277–78.

18. *Amor caritatis*: the difference between *amor*, *dilectio*, and *caritas*—three different words for love—is discussed in chap. 3 of part one. In this translation, I have always translated *caritas*, the highest form of love, by *charity*.

19. The author is here using *conscientia* simply as a synonym for knowledge or understanding, which enables us to distinguish good from evil. It was a term of rich meaning in the twelfth century and has been discussed in chap. 1 of part one.

20. For the concept, ultimately Plotinian, of God as *ubique praesens et ubique totus*, "everywhere present and everywhere whole," see Olivier du Roy, *L'Intelligence de la foi en la Trinité selon saint Augustin* (Paris: Études augustiniennes, 1966), 469–70; supplemented by James J. O'Donnell, *Augustine Confessions, Volume II: Commentary on Books 1–7* (Oxford: Oxford University Press, 1992), 22–23.

21. *Mens*: the highest part of the rational soul in which we are truly created *ad imaginem Dei*. It may sometimes be translated simply as "soul," but more often we need to distinguish the highest part of the soul from those parts that are lower. Sometimes we even need to distinguish the highest part of the highest part—the *apex mentis*—but that term does not appear in the *Meditationes*.

22. This sentence is a direct quotation from Augustine, *De Trinitate*, XIV. viii.11; PL 42:1044.

itself, understands itself, and loves itself, but because it is able to remember, understand, and love him by whom it was made, and when it does this, it becomes wise. There is nothing so similar to that Supreme Wisdom as the rational mind, which, by memory, understanding, and will, dwells in that ineffable Trinity; nor can it dwell therein unless it remembers it, understands it, and loves it. Let [the mind] remember God, therefore, to whose image it is made, understand and love him, and also worship him, with whom it can be forever blessed.[23] O blessed soul, with whom God finds rest, and in whose tabernacle he rests. Blessed is [that soul] that can say, "And he who created me rested in my tabernacle."[24] For he could not deny [that soul] heavenly rest.

3. Why, then, do we neglect ourselves, and seek God in these outward things, when he is with us if only we would be with him? He is indeed with us and in us,[25] though as yet only by faith, until we deserve to see him as he is.[26] "We know," says the Apostle, "that Christ dwells in our hearts by faith,"[27] for Christ is in faith, faith in the soul,[28] the soul in the heart, and the heart in the breast.[29] So it is that by faith I reflect on God the creator, adore him as redeemer, and await him as savior. I believe that I see him in all his creatures and that I have him within myself,

23. The whole section from "It follows, then, that the mind" to here is taken directly from Augustine, *De Trinitate*, XIV.xii.15; PL 42:1048.

24. Sir 24:12.

25. The author states that God is *apud*, *cum*, and *in* us.

26. 2 Cor 5:7: at present we walk *per fidem* and not *per speciem*.

27. Eph 3:17.

28. *Mens*: see n. 21 above.

29. This sentence, with a change in the order of the words, is taken from Peter Damian, *Sermo 58, In festo S. Andreae, sermo* 2; PL 144:830A: "The heart in the breast, the soul in the heart, the mind in the soul, faith in the mind, Christ in the faith. And this, I think, is what the Apostle means when he speaks of Christ 'dwelling in our hearts by faith.'" Nicholas of Clairvaux, in his own sermon for the feast of Saint Andrew, also borrows it from Peter Damian, but in his case, word for word: see Nicholas of Clairvaux, *In festo S. Andreae, sermo*; PL 184:1051A.

and, what is indescribably more joyful and blessed than all these things, that I know him in himself! For to know the Father and the Son, together with the Holy Spirit, is life eternal,[30] perfect bliss, and supreme delight.

The eye has not seen, nor the ear heard, nor has the human heart ever conceived[31] how much illumination, how much sweetness, and how much joy awaits us in that vision when we shall see God face to face.[32] For he is the light of those who are enlightened, rest for those who are weary,[33] the homeland of those on a journey, the life of those who live, the crown of those who conquer.[34]

Thus I find in my mind a certain image of that supreme Trinity, and to that supreme Trinity, by reflecting upon it, by examining it, and by loving it so as to remember it, delight in it, and embrace and contemplate[35] it, I should dedicate the whole of my life. The mind is an image of God,[36] in which are three things, namely, memory, understanding, and will. To memory we attribute all the things we know, even though we do not always have them in mind. To understanding we attribute all those things that, by thinking [about them], we find to be true, and that we also commit to memory. To will [we attribute] all the things we long for, having known and understood them to be good and true. By memory, we are like the Father, by understanding like the Son, and by will, like the Holy Spirit. There is nothing is us more similar to the

---

30. See John 17:3.

31. 1 Cor 2:9.

32. Gen 32:30.

33. Matt 11:28.

34. This sentence is taken directly from Augustine, *Quaestionum evangeliorum lib.* 2, *quaest.* 39; PL 35:1354.

35. *Contempler*: the first-person active subjunctive of *contemplor*: what the author means by "contemplating" is discussed in chap. 1 of part one.

36. *Mens imago Dei est.* We cannot translate this as "the mind is *the* image of God," since Christ alone is the image and we are made *to* the image, *ad imaginem.* We may, however, translate it as "the mind is *an* image is God," as I have done here, even if it is a very distant image.

Spirit than will or love or dilection,[37] which is a superior form of will.[38] For love is the gift of God,[39] so that there is nothing more excellent than this gift of God. For love, which is from God and is God,[40] is properly called the Holy Spirit, through whom the charity of God is poured forth in our hearts,[41] through whom the whole Trinity dwells within us.

37. The author here distinguishes *amor* from *dilectio*, which is why I have used the obsolete English word *dilection*. See n. 18 above.

38. The author is here directly dependent on Augustine, *De Trinitate*, XV.xxi.41; PL 42:1089, but the actual expression *excellentior voluntas* appears nowhere else in the Patrologia Latina. See further Étienne Gilson, trans. L. E. M. Lynch, *The Christian Philosophy of Saint Augustine* (New York: Vintage Books, 1967), 133, 162.

39. *Dilectio namque donum Dei est.* See the discussion in Augustine, *De Trinitate*, XV.xvii.28–31; PL 42:1080–82.

40. 1 John 4:7 states that *caritas* is "from God" (*ex Deo*), and the Vulgate text of 1 John 4:8, that *caritas* is God (*Deus caritas est*). Ps.-Bernard, however, follows Augustine here and uses *dilectio*, not *caritas*.

41. Rom 5:5.

CHAPTER TWO[42]

On Human Misery, the Horror of Death, and the Severity of the Supreme Judge

4. In my outer body, I come from those [first] parents who condemned me before they gave me birth. Sinners themselves, they have begotten in their sin a sinner and have nourished him with sin. Wretches have brought forth a wretch into the wretched light. Nothing have I from them save wretchedness and sin, and this corruptible body I carry about.[43] Truly, I hasten towards those who, by bodily death, have departed from here, and when I look on their tombs, I find in them nothing but ashes and worms, stench and horror. What I am, they have been, and what they are, I shall be.[44] What am I? A human being [born] from liquid moisture.[45] For

42. After the optimism of the first chapter, dealing with our creation *ad imaginem Dei*, we now turn to the depressing topic of the lost likeness.

43. From the beginning of this paragraph to here, the author is dependent on Bernard, *Epistola* 111.1; SBOp 7:283–84. At its basis is the Augustinian doctrine of total human depravity, in both Original Sin and Original Guilt, inherited by all of us from Adam "in whom all sinned." This is discussed in chap. 3 of part one. See also n. 66 below.

44. *Quod ego sum, ipsi fuerunt; et quod ipsi sunt, ego ero*. This is discussed in chap. 4 of part one.

45. For the expression *humore liquido*, see Hugh of Saint-Victor, *Didascalicon*, I.2; PL 176:742B.

at the moment of conception, I was conceived from human seed, and then that froth coagulated,[46] increased a little, and became flesh. After that, weeping and wailing, I was delivered into the exile of this world,[47] and behold! I am now dying, full of wickedness and abominations. And now, even now, I shall be brought before a severe Judge to render an account for what I have done.

Woe to me, wretch that I am, when that Day of Judgment shall come and the books are opened[48] in which everything I have done and thought will be read out and displayed before the Lord. Then, with head bowed low because of the confusion of my guilty conscience, I shall stand, trembling and anxious, before the Lord in Judgment, recalling all the wicked deeds I have ever committed. And when it is said of me, "Behold the man and his deeds!"[49] I shall bring back before my eyes all my sins and transgressions. For by some divine power, it is ordained that the good and evil deeds of every person are recalled to memory and are seen with miraculous speed by the gaze of the mind so that the knowledge [of them] may accuse or acquit one's conscience, and in this way, at one and the same time, they shall be judged both individually and altogether:[50]

> Each will make a judgment of his own deeds,
> And all the secrets of all shall be displayed to all.[51]

46. See Job 10:10.

47. The expression *hujus mundi exsilium* or *exsilium hujus mundi* is fairly common among patristic writers.

48. Rev 20:12.

49. *Ecce homo et opera ejus*: see Gaudentius of Brescia, Sermo 13; PL 20:942C, and the accompanying note. The same phrase appears in a number of works by and attributed to Ambrose of Milan and Jerome.

50. This entire sentence is taken directly from Augustine, *De civitate Dei*, XX.14; PL 41:679.

51. These two hexameters appear to come from two quite different poems. For the first (anonymous) line, *Judicium faciet gestorum quisque suorum*, see Walther, *Initia*, 9920, which is not of much help, and must be supplemented by the important discussion in Bultot, "Les 'Meditationes,'" 275. The second line,

For what now we are ashamed to confess will then be revealed to all, and everything we have cloaked here by dissimulation will there be burned up by an avenging flame:

A raging fire will everywhere reign unbridled.[52]

The longer God waits for us to amend [our lives], the more strictly will he judge us if we have neglected to do so.

5. Why, then, do we so prize this life in which the longer we live, the more we sin?[53] The longer our life, the more numerous our faults. Evils increase daily, and good things disappear. We constantly alternate between prosperity and adversity, and we do not know when we shall die. For just as a blazing star shoots swiftly across the sky and suddenly dies out, and just as a flaming spark is suddenly extinguished and reduced to ashes,

So we may see this life swiftly ended.[54]

For when someone lingers in this world, happily and with the utmost joy, thinking he will live long,

And plans to do many things over a long period,[55]

Cunctaque cunctorum cunctis arcana patebunt, is from Bede's well-known poem *De die judicii* (Walther, *Initia*, 9156); PL 94:635D. The problem of the verses that appear in the *Meditationes* is discussed in chap. 2 of part one.

52. *Ignis ubique ferox ruptis regnabit habenis.* This is also a line from Bede's poem *De die judicii* (Walther, *Initia*, 9156), and appears five lines further on from the line cited in the note immediately above. For *Ignis ubique ferox*, the text in PL 94:635D reads *Ignis ubique suis*.

53. This first sentence is borrowed from Ambrose, *De bono mortis*, ii.6; PL 14:542AB.

54. *Sic cito finitam datur istam cernere vitam.* Neither this line, nor any significant part of it, is recorded in Walther, PL, SCO, LLT (Series A and B), or PHI.

55. *Ac multa in longum disponit tempus agenda.* As with the line quoted in the note immediately above, neither this line, nor any significant part of it, is recorded in Walther, PL, or any of the standard data bases.

he is suddenly snatched away by death, and his soul is unexpectedly taken from his body.[56] But it is with great dread and much
grief that a soul is separated from the body, for angels come to take
it and bring it before the Judgment seat of the terrible Judge! And
then, remembering all the good and evil deeds it did by night and
day, [the soul] trembles and tries to flee and seek a truce, saying,
"Give me but the space of one hour!"

But then its deeds, speaking, as it were, all together, say: "You
committed us! We are your deeds! We shall not leave you, but will
be with you always and will go with you to Judgment!"[57] The vices,
too, will accuse the soul with many and manifold sins and will
invent many false testimonies against it, even though those that are
true can be quite sufficient for its damnation. Demons will terrify
it with their terrible faces and horrifying appearance:[58] they will
pursue it with great fury and seize it, terribly and horribly, seeking
to keep it and possess it, unless there be someone to rescue it.[59]

Then the soul, finding its eyes and mouth closed, together with
the other bodily senses by which it used to go forth and take
its pleasure in outward things, returns to itself, and seeing itself
alone and naked, shaking in great dread, it grows faint in itself in
despair and falls below itself. And because it forsook the love[60]
of God for the love of the world and the delights of the flesh, it
will be forsaken by God, wretched in its hour of greatest need,
and delivered to the demons to be tormented in hell.

56. See Luke 12:19-20.

57. The entire passage from "But it is with great dread" to here is taken
directly from either *ps.*-Augustine, *De rectitudine catholicae conversationis*,
21; PL 40:1183–84, or Ouen (Audoenus) of Rouen, *Life of St Eligius of Noyon*
(BHL 2474) xv; PL 87:543BC. Audoenus died in 684, but it is not certain that
he wrote the *Vita*. This issue is discussed in chap. 2 of part one.

58. The horrible faces of demons also appear in Bernard's sermon 42.6 *de
diversis*; SBOp 6/1:259, a sermon that has certainly influenced *ps.*-Bernard's
conception of hell.

59. Ps 70:11.

60. Here and five words further on, the word for love is the generic *amor*.

6.[61] Thus, on a day of which he is ignorant and at a time he does not know, the soul of a sinner is snatched away by death and separated from the body. It passes on, full of miseries, trembling and sorrowful, and since it has no excuse to offer for its sins, it pines away and is terrified to appear before God.

[The soul] is stricken with great horror and tossed about by the tempests of a multitude of thoughts, for at the imminent dissolution of the flesh, when all other things have been removed, it considers itself and that end to which it is approaching, and after a little while, it finds that which cannot be altered for all eternity. It now considers clearly how strict is the eternal Judge who is coming and, before the severity of such justice, what account it may give for its life. [The soul] may have avoided all those deeds that it could understand [should be avoided], yet since it is about to come before so strict a judge, it fears those that, in itself, it does not understand [should be avoided].[62] Its fear increases when it considers the fact that it could never tread the paths of this life without fault, nor that it ever lived commendably, without any fault, if it be judged without mercy.[63] For who can count how many evil deeds are committed at every moment, and how many good deeds we fail to do? For just as committing evil deeds is sin, so the omitting of good deeds is a fault.

But what a heavy loss it is when we neither do good deeds nor think about good deeds but, instead, let our hearts wander about among things that are empty and useless. Yet it is very difficult to control the heart and keep it free from every unlawful thought, and it is equally difficult to pursue worldly occupations without sinning. For this reason, no one is able to judge and understand

---

61. The whole of §6 is heavily indebted to Gregory the Great's *Moralia* on the book of Job. Specific details will be found in nn. 62–64 below.

62. The section from "It now considers clearly" to here is taken directly from Gregory the Great, *Moralia in librum Job*, XXIV.xi.32; PL 76:305A.

63. This sentence is taken directly from Gregory the Great, *Moralia in librum Job*, XXIV.xi.33; PL 76:306A.

oneself perfectly, but being busied with many thoughts, we remain in a certain way unknown to ourselves and are altogether ignorant of what we condone. Thus, when our end is at hand, we are deeply afraid in a more subtle way,[64] for although we remember that we have omitted nothing that we know about, we dread [the consequences] of the things we do not know.

64. Gregory the Great, *Moralia in librum Job*, XXIV.xi.32; PL 76:305D.

CHAPTER THREE

Of the Dignity of the Soul and the Baseness of the Body

7. O soul, bearing the seal of God's image, adorned with his likeness, betrothed [to him] by faith, endowed with his spirit, redeemed by his blood, ranked with his angels,[65] capable of blessedness, heir of goodness, participating in reason, what have you to do with the flesh from which you suffer so many things? Because of the flesh, the sins of others are imputed to you,[66] and your virtues are like the rag of a menstruous woman,[67] and you yourself are

65. Up to this point, this sentence appears in almost identical form in *ps.*-Augustine, *Manuale*, 24; PL 40:961; *ps.*-Anselm of Canterbury, *Meditatio super Miserere*, 27; PL 158:840A; and *ps.*-Hugh of Saint-Victor, *De anima*, IV.11; PL 177:182CD. I have no idea which came first.

66. We are back with the Augustinian doctrine of Original Sin. The "others" are Adam and Eve, and since the whole human race was potentially present in them, when they sinned, we sinned. Or, as the author puts it, their sin was imputed to us who were not there to sin at the time. Furthermore, since, in Augustine's view, Original Sin was transmitted by the actual act of sexual intercourse, it follows that any children conceived by the processes of human reproduction would enter this world stained and corrupted with sin, though they had not yet committed any sin themselves. See further David N. Bell, *A Cloud of Witnesses: An Introduction to the Development of Christian Doctrine to AD 500*, 2nd ed., CS 218 (Kalamazoo, MI: Cistercian Publications, 2007), 162–63, and n. 43 above.

67. Isa 64:6.

brought to nothing and accounted as nothing and worthless. The flesh, with which you have such great intimacy, is nothing but froth made flesh, clad in frail beauty, but the time will come when it will be a wretched and stinking corpse and food for worms. For however much you cosset it, it remains but flesh.

If you examine carefully what comes out of the mouth and nose and other bodily orifices, you will never have seen a more filthy heap of dung. If you wish to total up each and every one of its miseries, you will find it burdened with sins, entangled in wickedness, itching for fleshly pleasures, possessed by passions, polluted by indecent thoughts, ever prone to wickedness, ready for every kind of vice, and filled with every disorder and degradation. On account of the flesh, humankind is made as if worthless,[68] for from [the flesh] derives the vice of concupiscence by which it is held captive and made crooked,[69] that it may love worthless things and work iniquity.

8. Take note, you men and women, of what you were before your birth, what you are from your birth to your death, and what you will be after this life. There was a time when you did not exist. After that you were made from lowly matter and wrapped in a most lowly covering and nourished by menstrual blood in your mother's womb,[70] and your clothing was a second-hand skin.

> Thus clad and adorned you came to us,
> Nor did you remember how lowly was your origin.

---

68. Ps 143:4.

69. *Incurvatur*: the author is here echoing Bernard's important distinction between *anima recta* and *anima curva*: "Rejecting the divine for the sake of the earthly, man accordingly demands his own portion in preference to God's, and, in so doing, loses his upright status, stoops, bends down, turns away from heaven to which God had erected him, to bow himself down to earth to which his animal nature attracts him. From 'recta', which once it was, the soul has now become 'curva'" (Étienne Gilson, trans. A. H. C. Downes, *The Mystical Theology of Saint Bernard* [London: Sheed and Ward, 1940; repr. Kalamazoo, MI: Cistercian Publications, 1990], 53–54).

70. See Isidore of Seville, *Etymologiarum liber*, XI,i,139; PL 82:414B.

Beauty, popularity, youthful enthusiasm, and riches
Have stolen from you the knowledge of what a human being is.[71]

A human being is nothing but stinking sperm, a sack of shit, and food for worms.[72]

After the human the worm. After the worm, stench and horror.
Thus is each person turned into a non-person.[73]

So why are you proud, you men and women, considering that you were vile sperm and coagulated blood in the womb? And then, after being exposed to the miseries of this life and to sin, you will be a worm and food for worms in the grave. Why are you proud, you who are dust and ashes,[74] you who were conceived in shame[75] and born in misery to live in pain and die in anguish?

71. Neither the first two lines—*Sic indutus et ornatus progressus es ad nos, / Nec memor es quam sit vilis origo tui*—nor any significant part of them is recorded in Walther, PL, or any of the standard data bases. The second two lines, however—*Forma, favor populi, fervor juvenilis, opesque? / Subripuere tibi noscere quid sit homo*—are well known: see Walther, *Initia*, 6757; and Bultot, "Les 'Meditationes,'" 276.

72. See *ps.*-Augustine, *Sermo 48 ad fratres in eremo commorantes*; PL 40:1331.

73. For this distich and that which follows a few lines further on (n. 76 below), see the long discussion in Bultot, "Les 'Meditationes,'" 276–81. The second distich does not appear in all the manuscripts, and the author suggests that it came not from the pen of *ps.*-Bernard but was a marginal addition by an unknown reader that came to be incorporated into the text at a later date. He associates both distichs with the work of Adam of Saint-Victor. The exact form of the first distich, however—*Post hominem vermis, post vermem fetor et horror. / Sic in non hominem vertitur omnis homo*—does not appear in Adam and is not recorded in Walther, PL, or any of the standard data bases. For further discussion of this matter, see chap. 2 of part one.

74. Gen 18:27.

75. Ps 50:7.

> Why are men and women proud, whose conception is
> shameful,
> Whose birth is pain, whose life is trouble, and whose death
> is inevitable?[76]

Why do you flatter and adorn your flesh with costly things when, after a few days, it will be devoured by worms in the tomb? Yet you fail to adorn your soul with good works, though it must be brought before God and his angels in heaven.[77] Why do you despise your soul and put the flesh before it? It is a grave abuse for the mistress to serve and the servant to rule.[78] The whole of this world is not worth the price of a single soul.[79] Not for the whole world did God wish to give up his soul, yet he gave it up for the human soul.[80] Thus the price of a soul that could be redeemed only by the blood of Christ[81] is higher [than that of the whole world].

So what will you give in exchange for your soul,[82] you who give it away for nothing? Did not the Son of God, when he was in the bosom of the Father,[83] descend from his royal throne for your soul's sake,[84] to free it from the power of the devil? When he saw

76. *Unde superbit homo, cujus conceptio culpa, / Nasci poena, labor vita, necesse mori.* These two lines do not appear in all the manuscripts, and Bultot suggests that they were a later marginal addition incorporated into the text by some copyist: see n. 73 above. The distich itself is well known and is listed in Walther, *Initia*, 19639, who attributes it to Hildebert of Lavardin. This attribution is doubtful: see Bultot, "Les 'Meditationes,'" 282, n. 2. The same distich, in exactly this form, also appears in the *De interiori domo*, xxviii.61; PL 184:538C, and in a very slightly different form in the *De spiritu et anima*, 51; PL 40:817.

77. The last part of this sentence may be dependent on Anselm of Canterbury: see PL 158:1054B.

78. See Prov 30:22–23.

79. See Mark 8:36; Matt 16:26.

80. I.e. Christ did not die to save the world, but to save human souls.

81. See Eph 1:7.

82. Mark 8:37; Matt 16:26.

83. John 1:18.

84. Wis 18:15.

it ensnared in the bonds of sinners[85] and already handed over to the demons to be condemned to eternal death, he wept over it,[86] [a soul] that did not know how to weep over itself. But not only did he weep; he even allowed himself up to be killed so that he might redeem it with the precious price of his own blood.[87]

Behold, mortal, for you was such a victim sacrificed![88]

9. Acknowledge, then, you men and women, how noble is your soul, and how grievous were its wounds for which it was needful that Christ the Lord be wounded. If these wounds had not been [so serious as to lead] to death, and eternal death at that, the Son of God would never have died to heal them. Do not then denigrate the passion of your own soul, for which you see such great compassion shown by so great a Majesty.[89] He himself shed tears for you: do you, then, water your bed night after night with compunction of heart and constant tears.[90] He himself poured forth his blood for you:[91] do you, then, pour forth your own by daily treating your body harshly, for if you cannot offer it up all at once for Christ, then at least offer it up by a milder if longer martyrdom.[92] Take no notice of what the flesh wants, but what the spirit needs. Then it shall be glorious when it returns to its God, provided it brings with it no bodily sin and has wiped away every filthy stain.

85. Prov 5:22.

86. Luke 19:41.

87. See Acts 20:28.

88. *Aspice, mortalis, pro te datur hostia talis*: Walther, *Initia*, 1584. See also Bultot, "Les 'Meditationes,' " 275.

89. The section from the beginning of §9 to here is taken directly from Bernard, *In nativitate Domini, sermo* 3.4; SBOp 4:261. As usual, some of it is quoted verbatim, some of it paraphrased, and so on.

90. See Ps 6:7. The expression *compunctio cordis* is very common, but the author is here following Bernard: see n. 92 below.

91. See Matt 26:28.

92. The section from "do you, then, water your bed" to here is taken directly from Bernard, *In octava Paschae, sermo* 1.7; SBOp 5:116.

If you say, "This is too hard! I can't despise the world and hate my own flesh!" then tell me, where now are those who loved the world, those who were with us just a little while ago? Nothing remains of them but ashes and worms! Pay careful attention to what they are, or, rather, what they were. They were people just like you: they ate, they drank, they laughed, they spent their days in good cheer, and in a moment they went down into hell![93] Here, their flesh is for the worms. There, their soul is destined for the fire, until [body and soul] are once again joined together in unhappy company, and together, just as they were partners in wickedness, they shall both be covered by the everlasting flames. One punishment involves both, whom one love of sin bound together.[94] What did they gain by all this vain glory, this fleeting joy, this worldly power, these pleasures of the flesh, these deceptive riches, these great households, these evil lusts? Where now are their laughter, their jokes, their boasting, their pride? From so much pleasure, so much sorrow! After so little enjoyment, what grievous misery! From all that revelling, they have fallen into great misery, into profound ruin and great torment.

10. What happened to them can also happen to you because you are a human being: earthly from the earth,[95] slime from slime.[96] Of the earth[97] you are, from the earth you live, and to the earth you will return when that last day comes—and it will come suddenly, perhaps today! That you will die is certain. What is uncertain is when, how, or where. Since death awaits you everywhere, you,

93. Job 21:13.

94. The last three sentences are taken directly from Bernard, *De diversis, sermo* 19.1; SBOp 6/1:162.

95. There is a play on words here: *homo de humo*.

96. *Limus de limo*: see Gen 2:7, which states that the Lord God created human beings *de limo terrae*, "from the slime of the earth." We discussed this in chap. 3 of part one.

97. The author now changes to the more usual word *terra*, echoing John 3:31.

too, if you are wise, will await it everywhere.[98] If you follow the flesh, you will be punished in the flesh; if you take delight in the flesh, you will be tormented in the flesh. If you need fine clothes, then instead of your fancy garments, moths shall be spread under you and worms shall be your covering.[99] For the only thing that the justice of God can judge is what our actions deserve. Those who love the world more than God, life in the world more than the cloister,[100] gluttony more than abstinence, lechery more than chastity, follow the devil and go with him into eternal torment.

Can you imagine what sorrow there will be then, what grief, what heartache, when the wicked shall be separated from the company of the saints and the vision of God? When they shall be handed over into the power of the demons and go with them into everlasting fire where they shall be forever in grief and lamentation? Exiled far from the blessed region of Paradise, they are tormented in hell forever, never to see the light, never to find relief, but to be tormented in hell for thousands upon thousands of years. From there they are never released, while those who torment them are never wearied and those who are tormented never die. For just as the fire that consumes them always keeps them alive, so the torments are done in such a way that they are always renewed.

Everyone will suffer the punishment of hell according to the nature of the sin [they have committed], and those who are guilty of similar sins will be joined with their like to be tormented.

98. These last three sentences also appear in the *De spiritu et anima*, 31; PL 40:800. The last sentence, however, reading *Quoniam mors ubique te exspectat, tu quoque, si sapiens fueris, ubique eam exspectabis*, is a paraphrase of L. Annaeus Seneca (Seneca the Younger), *Epistulae morales ad Lucilium*, *Ep*. III.26.7, which reads *Incertum est quo loco te mors exspectet; itaque tu illam omni loco exspecta*, "It is uncertain in what place death awaits you, so await it in every place." It appears in precisely this form in *ps*.-Augustine, *Formula honestae vitae*, the end of the last chapter; PL 184:1170D.

99. Isa 14:11.

100. *Saeculum quam claustrum*: it will be remembered that the author of the *Meditationes* was a monk, almost certainly a Cistercian.

Nothing will be heard there save weeping and wailing, groans and shrieks, lamentation and the gnashing of teeth.[101] Nothing will be seen there, save worms, the hideous faces of the torturers, and the foulest demonic monsters.

> Savage worms will eat up your very heart,
> From this comes anguish, and from that dread, groans, stupor, and terrible fear.[102]

The wretched will burn in eternal flames for ever and ever. In the flesh they will be tormented by fire, in the spirit by the worm of their conscience.[103] There, there will be unendurable pain, terrible fear, an intolerable stink, and the death of both body and soul without hope of mercy or reprieve. For thus shall they die, yet forever remain alive, and so shall they remain alive, yet forever die.[104] In this way, the soul of the sinner is either tormented in hell for its sins or placed in Paradise for its good merits.

So let us now choose one of the two: either to be tormented with the wicked or to rejoice forever with the saints. Good and evil, life and death, are set before us,[105] so that we may hold out our hand to whichever we want! If the torments don't scare us, the rewards at least might entice us!

101. This entire paragraph, from "Can you imagine" to here, has been taken directly from either *ps.*-Augustine, *De rectitudine catholicae conversationis*, 23; PL 40:1186; or Ouen (Audoenus) of Rouen, *Life of St Eligius of Noyon* (BHL 2474) xv; PL 87:546CD. See also n. 57 above. The weeping and gnashing of teeth have been taken from Matt 8:12 and Luke 13:28.

102. *Vermes crudeles mordebunt intima cordis: / Hinc dolor, inde pavor, gemitus, stupor, et timor horrens.* These are two lines from Bede's poem *De die judicii.* The first appears at PL 94:636A, reading *vermes scelerum* for *vermes crudeles*; the second thirty-one lines further on at PL 94:636C, reading *stridor* for *stupor.*

103. This sentence has been taken from Hugh of Saint-Victor, *De sacramentis christianae fidei*, II.xvi.5; PL 178:588AB.

104. This sentence, with minor variations, has been taken directly from Bernard, *De diversis, sermo* 19.1; SBOp 6/1:162.

105. See Deut 30:15.

CHAPTER FOUR

Of the Reward
of the Heavenly Homeland

11. The reward is to see God,[106] to live with God, to live from God, to be with God, to be in God, who will be all in all:[107] to possess God, who is the Supreme Good.[108] And where there is the Supreme God, there is supreme happiness, supreme delight, true freedom, perfect charity, eternal security, and secure eternity.[109] There is true joy, full knowledge, all beauty and all blessedness:

> There is peace, godliness, goodness, light, virtue, integrity,
> Joy, gladness, sweetness, everlasting life.
> Glory, praise, rest, love, and sweet agreement.[110]

106. See Augustine, *Contra Maximinum*, II.ix.1; PL 42:763: "The eternal reward of the faithful is to see God."

107. 1 Cor 15:28.

108. The expression *summum bonum* appears to have originated with Cicero, but in the Christian tradition it is especially associated with Augustine. In his early works, he tended to use it to describe the highest human happiness, but in all the works of his maturity, it is synonymous with God. Witness the beginning of his *De natura boni*: *Deus summum bonum et incommutabile, a quo caetera omnia bona spiritualia et corporalia. Summum bonum quo superius non est, Deus est* (*De natura boni*, 1; PL 42:551).

109. See *ps.*-Gregory the Great, *Expositio in septem psalmi poenitentiales*, 19; PL 79:658AB.

110. *Est ibi pax, pietas, bonitas, lux, virtus, honestas, / Gaudia, laetitiae, dulcedo, vita perennis. / Gloria, laus, requies, amor, et concordia dulcis*: see Walther, *Initia*, 5698, and Bultot, "Les 'Meditationes,'" 282.

Thus, with God, will they be blessed in whose conscience no sin is found. They will see God when they will; they will possess him when they please; they will enjoy him in happiness. They will flourish in eternity, they will shine in truth, they will rejoice in goodness. Just as they will have endless existence, so they will have ease of knowledge and joy in repose.[111] They will be citizens of that holy city of which the angels are citizens, God the Father its temple, his Son its splendor, and the Holy Spirit its charity.[112] O heavenly city! Safest of dwellings, fruitful and spacious homeland, that contains everything that can offer delight: a people without complaint, inhabitants at peace, and the men and women there wanting for nothing.[113] "What glorious things are said of you, city of God! It is as if all joy dwells in you!"[114] All rejoice in joy and exultation: all delight in God, whose countenance is lovely, whose face is beautiful, whose words are sweet. He is delightful to see, sweet to possess, a pleasure to enjoy. He pleases by himself alone, and in himself he is all that we need for what is due to us, and all that we need for our reward. We need seek nothing other than him, for all that can be desired is found in him. It is always a joy to see him, to possess him always, always to find our delight in him and enjoy him.[115] In him our understanding is enlightened and our yearning purified, both for knowing and for loving the truth. For this is the whole of human good, namely, to know and love the Creator.[116]

111. For this sentence, see Augustine, *De civitate Dei*, XI.31; PL 41:344.

112. For Augustine's view of the Holy Spirit as *caritas*, the mutual love of Father and Son, see chap. 3 of part one.

113. The section from "O heavenly city!" to here is based on Cassiodorus, *De anima*, 12; PL 70:1303D.

114. Ps 86:3, 7.

115. The whole section from "All rejoice in joy" to here is directly paralleled in *De spiritu et anima*, 55; PL 40:821.

116. *Et hoc est totum bonum hominum, nosse scilicet et amare Creatorem suum.* We may compare *ps.*-Hugh of Saint-Victor, *Miscellanea*, I, tit. 103; PL 177:535B: *Hoc enim totum bonum est hominis cognoscere et amare Creatorem suum.*

12. What madness, then, drives us to thirst for the wormwood of the vices, to seek shipwreck in this world, to suffer the misfortunes of this fleeting life, and to endure the dominion of its wicked tyranny? Should we not rather flee to the happiness of the saints, the company of the angels,[117] the feast day of the joys above, and the pleasure of the contemplative life,[118] so that we may enter the kingdom of the Lord and see those superabundant riches of his goodness?[119] There we will be at rest, and we will see how sweet the Lord is,[120] and how great is the abundance of his sweetness.[121] We will see the beauty of his glory, the splendor of his saints, and the honor of his royal power. We will understand the power of the Father, the wisdom of the Son, and the most bountiful mercy of the Holy Spirit,[122] and in this way we will have knowledge of that supreme Trinity.

Now we see bodies by means of the body, and we discern [mental] images of bodies by means of the spirit.[123] But then, indeed, we shall see the Trinity itself with the pure sight of the mind. O blessed vision! To see God in himself, to see him in us and us in him in happy bliss and blissful happiness. Whatever we desire, we shall wholly possess, desiring nothing more; and whatever we see we shall love, being blessed by that love itself, blessed by the delight of love and

---

117. The section from the beginning of this paragraph to here is taken directly from *ps.*-Julian of Toledo, *In Nahum*, 22; PL 96:717D–18A. This commentary is certainly not by Julian and may come from Victorine circles. The manuscript evidence seems to me to point to a date prior to that of the *Meditationes*, so that *ps.*-Bernard has borrowed from *ps.*-Julian, and not the other way round.

118. *Ps.*-Julian of Toledo, *In Nahum*, 29; PL 96:721C.

119. Eph 2:7.

120. Ps 33:9.

121. Ps 30:20.

122. *Ps.*-Julian of Toledo, *In Nahum*, 29; PL 96:721D.

123. We may compare Candidus of Fulda, *Epistola*, 6; PL 106:106B, but the thought is Augustinian. I suspect, however, though I cannot quite prove it, that this and the following sentence are echoing Boethius: see chap. 3, n. 14.

the sweetness of contemplation. This[124] will be the consummation of that contemplation, this will be the consummation of that happiness, when true divinity will be understood in its pure essence, and the incomprehensible Trinity comprehended therein. The mysteries of divinity shall be revealed; God will be seen and loved. And this vision and delight, filling and satisfying the whole of the human heart, will be the complete consummation of that blessedness.

There will be one language for all, unwearied rejoicing, one state of mind, eternal love. Truth will be laid open, charity will be complete, and there will be perfect harmony between body and soul. Humanity, glorified, shall shine like the sun,[125] and the fellowship of flesh and spirit will be peaceful and harmonious. There will be one joy for angels and humankind, one conversation, one banquet. Love shall not languish,[126] nor charity melt away. Since all good things will be there, no one will suffer any delay [in receiving them], for the beatific presence of the Divine Majesty will be all things for all,[127] and omnipotence, wisdom, peace, righteousness, and understanding will be common to all. In that peace there will be no diversity of language, but a peaceful and harmonious concord of ways of life and thought. In the torrent of that pleasure,[128] there will be so much happiness, so complete and abundant, that there will be no desire for anything else. For there, there will be an abundance of happiness, preeminent glory, superabundant joy.

13. But who is ready for this? Only the true penitent, someone good and obedient, a loving friend, a faithful servant.[129] A true penitent is always laboring and grieving: he grieves over what is

---

124. The whole section, from here to the very end of this paragraph and the beginning of §13, is taken directly from Arnold of Bonneval, *De operibus sex dierum*; PL 189:1551B–52C. Some of it is quoted verbatim, some of it is paraphrased, and *ps.*-Bernard has made some additions.

125. Matt 13:43.

126. See Song 2:5; 5:8.

127. 1 Cor 9:22.

128. Ps 35:9.

129. Matt 24:45.

past; he labors to avoid future [perils]. For true penitence[130] is to grieve for one's sins without ever ceasing, and to bewail what we have committed in such a way as never again to commit the things we have bewailed! Those who continue to do that of which they repent are scoffers, not true penitents. Thus, if you want to be a true penitent, stop sinning, and do not sin any more! For repentance is vain if it is defiled by some subsequent sin.[131]

Every good and obedient person gives up what he himself wants or does not want so that he can say, "My heart is ready, O God, my heart is ready!":[132] ready to do whatever you command, ready to obey you at a nod or even sooner, ready to be at your service, to attend to my neighbor, to watch over myself, and to find repose in the contemplation of heavenly things.

A loving friend is attentive to all and a burden to none. He is attentive to all because he is devoted to God, kind towards his neighbor, and self-controlled with regard to the world: a servant of the Lord, a friend to his neighbor, a master of the world. He has things above him for his joy, things equal to him for fellowship, things below him at his service. He is a burden to none[133] but makes use of things below him to profit things in the middle and to honor the things above. Following the higher things, he draws those that are lower after him, being possessed by the former and possessing the latter.[134]

130. Or "true repentance": *poenitentia* can mean penitence or repentance, or both at the same time.

131. This whole paragraph, from "A true penitent" to here, is taken from Hugh of Saint-Victor, *Summa sententiarum*, VI.12; PL 176:149D–50A. The last sentence, *inanis est poenitentia quam sequens coinquinat culpa*, is correctly attributed by Hugh to Isidore of Seville: see Isidore of Seville, *Synonyma*, I.77; PL 83:845A. One also finds it attributed to Augustine and Gratian.

132. Ps 107:2.

133. 2 Cor 11:9.

134. This paragraph, with its description of the *amabilis socius*, is taken directly from Guigo I of la Chartreuse, *Meditationes*,19; PL 153:629CD. Some of it is quoted verbatim, some of it is paraphrased, and there are a few minor additions.

He is a faithful servant in the contemplation of God and keeping careful watch over himself. First of all, then, take the greatest care to keep careful watch over yourself. Then, realizing that you can never by your own efforts keep a sufficient watch over yourself, implore [the aid of] the divine mercy. And again, so that you may contemplate in yourself the good, well-pleasing, and perfect will of your Creator, beseech his angels to guard you, and beg all those who now reign with Christ[135] [in heaven] to protect you. Pursue them individually, beseech each one, and call on them all together and say, "Have pity on me, my friends; you, at least, have pity on me!"[136] Take back your runaway slave, but [take him back] as your cousin and kinsman in the blood of the Redeemer.

See, a poor man stands at the door: he calls and knocks:[137] "Open to him who knocks and take him to your king! So prostrate before him may I tell him all my needs and all the miseries I suffer." Last, rededicate your heart and all that comes forth from it to him who is set over you.[138] Let no sin remain in you that is not blotted out by a complete confession.[139] Set Jesus Christ as a seal over your heart.[140] When Christ guards the door of the heart he is also the heart's doorkeeper,[141] so that the whole household of your heart must go in and out through him. As a consequence of this,

135. *Cum Christo regnantium*: a common phrase in patristic writings, based on 2 Tim 2:12.

136. Job 19:21.

137. See Rev 3:20.

138. *Praelato tuo*: on the term *praelatus*, see Giraud, *Spiritualité*, 168–69.

139. *Pura confessione*, "by pure confession." For the phrase *pura confessio*, see the *Regula ad virgines*, 16; PL 88:1066B. The writer, who is a priest, says considerably more about the importance of confession later on, and he makes it clear that if the confession is to be effective, it must be accurate, complete, and heartfelt. This is what he means by *purus*. Further on confession, see chap. 3 of part one.

140. Song 8:6.

141. *Cordis ostiarius*: this is the sole occurrence of this rather lovely title in the whole of the PL.

there are present thousands upon thousands of angels[142] keeping watch at the doors of your outward senses, so that no unwelcome stranger might dare to break through those terrible battle-lines, for the reverence they have for the doorkeeper and the guardianship of the angels.

142. See Heb 12:22.

CHAPTER FIVE

On the Daily Examination
of Oneself

14. Make a daily examination of your life, and be thorough in investigating whether you are as virtuous as you should be.[143] Take careful note of how much you advance [in virtue] and in how much you fall back, what you are like in your outward actions and what you are like in your inner feelings, how similar you are to God, and how dissimilar, how near to him or how far from him, not by any spatial distance, but by how you act and think. Strive to know yourself, for it is far better and far more praiseworthy if you know yourself than, if neglecting yourself, you know the courses of the stars,[144] the curative powers of herbs, the constitutions of men and women, the natures of animals, and have knowledge of all things in heaven and earth.[145]

143. *Integritatis tuae curiosus explorator vitam tuam in quotidiana discussione examina.* I have, for once, paraphrased this sentence to bring out the sense. What follows in this paragraph has been much influenced by Hugh of Saint-Victor, *De institutione novitiorum*, 9; PL 176:934AC, and parts of it appear in the *De spiritu et anima*, 51; PL 40:817.

144. Astrology was a standard part of medieval medicine.

145. See Wis 7:17-20. This whole sentence echoes Augustine, *De Trinitate*, IV, *proem.*; PL 42:885, but it is not a direct quotation.

Restore yourself to yourself, therefore, and if not always or often, at least from time to time. Control your longings, direct your actions, amend your ways. Let nothing disorderly remain in you. Put all your transgressions before your eyes. Set yourself up before yourself, as if before a stranger, and so mourn for yourself. Weep for your iniquities and sins by which you have offended God.[146] Tell him of your wretchedness, and make known to him the malice of your enemies. And when you humble yourself before him in tears, I beg you also to remember me.[147]

15. For ever since I knew you, I have loved you in Christ.[148] And I send up a remembrance of you to that place where every unlawful thought merits punishment, and every worthy one a reward.[149] For when I stand at the altar of God, a sinner yet a priest,[150] the memory of you is there with me. So if ever you have loved me,[151] you will do as much for me in return, and make me a part of your prayers. I would like to be present with you in your memory when you pour forth your devout prayers before God for yourself and for those who are dear to you.[152] Do not be surprised if I say "present with you,"[153] for if you love me, and love me

146. This idea will appear numerous times in the rest of the *Meditationes*. On the gift or grace of tears, see the discussion in chap. 4 of part one.

147. The *Meditationes* now become personal as the author speaks to the individual to whom they were addressed. He, too, was a monk, undoubtedly of the same order.

148. *In Christo diligo te*. The author uses the verb *diligere* here, which indicates a high form of love, or a love that is rightly directed. Any discussion of gay relationships here would be utter nonsense.

149. There seems to be an echo here of Hildebert of Lavardin, *Epistola* 122.2 to Bernard of Clairvaux; PL 182:267A.

150. *Sacerdos*: the word leaves no doubt as to the author's priestly status.

151. *Si me amaveris*: here he uses the generic verb *amare*.

152. "for those who are dear to you" translates *tuis familiaribus*. *Familiaris* here has a wider meaning than a family member or member of the household. It might simply be translated by "friends."

153. The entire section from here to the end of chap. five is dependent on Claudianus Mamertus, *De statu animae*, I.27; PL 53:736AC.

because I am the image of God, then I am just as present to you as you yourself are [present] to yourself. For whatever you are in your essence,[154] I am the same.

Every rational soul is an image of God.[155] Thus, whoever seeks the image of God in himself seeks his neighbor as much as himself, and whoever by seeking finds that image in himself recognizes it in every human being. For the intellect[156] is the very vision of the soul. If therefore you see yourself, you see me, who am nothing other than you! And if you love God, you love me as the image of God, and I, in loving God, love you! Thus, when we both seek one thing and press on towards one thing, we are always present to each other, but in God, in whom we love each other.[157]

154. *Substantialiter*: the author has taken the word directly from Claudianus Mamertus (PL 53:736A).

155. *Imago enim Dei est omnis anima rationalis*: this is taken directly from Claudianus Mamertus (PL 53:736B).

156. *Intellectus*: the word is that of Claudianus Mamertus (PL 53:736A).

157. We must remember that this remarkable doctrine is not that of *ps.*-Bernard, but of Claudianus Mamertus. See n. 153 above.

CHAPTER SIX

On the Need to Be Attentive at the Time of Prayer

16. When you go into a church to pray or sing praises, leave the tumult of your ever-changing thoughts[158] outside and completely forget all worldly cares so that you can be free for God alone. For it is impossible for us to talk to God at any time if, though [outwardly] silent, we are [inwardly] prattling away to the whole world. Pay heed to him, then, who pays heed to you;[159] listen to him speaking to you so that he might listen to you speaking to him. This will be so if, when divine praises are to be offered up, you are attentive to what you are doing with all due reverence and care, while paying careful heed to each and every word of divine Scripture.

I do not say that I myself [manage] to do this, but it is what I would like to do, and it grieves me when I have not done it, and it irks me when I do not do it. But you, on whom has been bestowed greater grace, incline the merciful ears of the Lord towards you with vows and devout prayers. With tears and sighs, beg him to

---

158. The expression *fluctuantium cogitationum tumultus* appears elsewhere only in Richard of Saint-Victor, *Benjamin major*, III.23; PL 196:132C. This is discussed in chap. 2 of part one.

159. *Intende ergo illi qui intendit tibi.* Precisely the same sentence appears in *ps.*-Augustine, *Manuale*, 24; PL 40:961.

have mercy on your mistakes, and, with spiritual songs,[160] praise
and glorify him in all his works. For there is no greater delight
for the citizens of the realms above than to see [this praise], and
nothing gives greater joy to the Supreme King, as he himself
bears witness: "The sacrifice of praise will glorify me."[161] Oh!
How happy you would be if with the eyes of the spirit you could
see but once how "the princes together with the singers go before,
in the midst of young women playing on tambourines!"[162] Then,
without any doubt, you would see with what attentiveness and
exultation they are there among the singers, attending those who
pray, being with those in meditation, giving support to those at
rest, governing those who provide and distribute [what is needed].
For the higher powers[, the angels,] love their fellow-citizens, and
for those who receive the inheritance of salvation,[163] they are eager
to rejoice with them, encourage them, instruct them, protect them,
and provide for them all.[164]

They all long for our arrival, since they look to us to restore the
ruins of their city.[165] They diligently seek and gladly hear good

160. Eph 5:19.
161. Ps 49:23.
162. Ps 67:26.
163. Heb 1:14.
164. With the exception of the first sentence, the whole of this paragraph has
been taken directly from Bernard's *Epistola* 78.6 to Suger of Saint-Denis; SBOp
7:205. The next three paragraphs, to the end of §16 and the first paragraph of
§17, are based on Bernard, *In vigilia nativitatis Domini, sermo* 2.6–8; SBOp
4:208–11. Some of this material is quoted verbatim, some of it is paraphrased,
some of it is omitted, and there are minor additions.
165. The background to this is the theory, probably put forward for the first
time by Augustine, that at the resurrection, the human bodies of those predestined
to be saved will be transformed into angelic bodies, and that as a consequence,
all the angels who fell with Lucifer will now be replaced by angelic human beings, or, as Augustine says in his *Enchiridion*, 61, "the ruins will be repaired"
(PL 40:260). Augustine's basis for this is Luke 20:36, where Christ states that in
the resurrection, those who are raised in glory will be *aequales angelis*, "equal
to the angels." The idea was then taken up by Gregory the Great and Anselm of
Canterbury, and by the time of the composition of the *Meditationes*, was stan-

things of us. They run anxiously to and fro as mediators between us and God, carrying most faithfully our sorrows to him and most devoutly bringing back his grace to us. They will not be ashamed to be our comrades who are already made our servants,[166] and when we turn to repentance, we give them cause to rejoice. So let us hasten, through them, to make their joy complete![167]

Woe to you, then, whoever you are, who wish to return to your vomit and go back to [wallowing in] your mud![168] Do you think that they will be well disposed to you on [the Day of] Judgment, those whom you would deprive of so much hoped-for joy? They rejoiced when we turned to the religious life,[169] as for those whom they saw called back from the very gates of hell. But what will happen if they see you draw back from the entrance to Paradise and go backwards again, you who already have one foot in heaven? For although their bodies were here below, yet their hearts were lifted up [to the Lord].[170]

17. Let us run, therefore, not with our bodily feet but with our mental yearnings, with our desires and longings, for it is not only the angels who await us, but the Creator of the angels. God the Father awaits us, as children and heirs, to put us in possession of

---

dard thinking in the West. See Vojtech Novotny, *Cur Homo? A History of the Thesis Concerning Man as a Replacement for Fallen Angels* (Charles University in Prague: Karolinum Press, 2014).

166. See Heb 1:14.

167. See John 15:11 and 16:24.

168. 2 Pet 2:22.

169. *Ad religionem. Religio,* in Medieval Latin, is a word of wide meaning. It can mean religion in general, the Christian religion in particular, religious belief, religious sentiment, religious faith, or the religious way of life, i.e., monasticism. It might also be translated by *piety* or *godliness*. The translation, therefore, depends on the context, but in this case *ps.*-Bernard has changed the authentic Bernard's *ad poenitentiam* to *ad religionem*, which seems to me to imply that he is speaking of the religious life. We may remember too that the author of the *Meditationes* is one monk writing to another.

170. See Col 3:1-2, and the *Sursum corda* in the Mass: V. *Sursum corda.* R. *Habere ad Dominum.*

all his goods.[171] The Son of God awaits us, as brothers and sisters and co-heirs,[172] that he might offer us up to his Father as the fruits of his birth[173] and the price of his blood. The Holy Spirit awaits us, for he himself is charity and benevolence, in whom we were predestined from all eternity.[174] Nor is there any doubt that he wishes what he has predestined to be accomplished. Thus, since the whole heavenly court awaits us and desires us, let us desire it with as much desire as we possibly can! For those who do not ardently desire to see [that court] will come to it in great embarrassment and shame. But those who dwell there by constant prayer and by continually thinking about it will make their way there untroubled and be received there with the greatest joy.

Wherever you may be, then, pray within yourself. If you are far from a place of prayer,[175] don't look for a place, because you yourself are the place! If you're in bed or anywhere else, pray, and there's your temple![176] We must pray often, and, with body bowed down, raise up our mind to God.[177] For just as there is not a single moment when we do not use and enjoy God's goodness and mercy, so there should not be a single moment when we do not have him present in our memory.[178]

171. See Matt 24:47.

172. Rom 8:17.

173. See Ps 106:37.

174. Eph 1:11.

175. *Si longe fueris ab oratorio.* Since this is probably a reference to the *Regula S. Benedicti*, 50, we might translate it more specifically as "if you are far from the abbey church."

176. There is a very close parallel to these last three sentences in the homily *de muliere Chananaea*, attributed to Lawrence of Novara. This is discussed in detail in chap. 2 of part one.

177. *Frequenter orandum, et flexo corpore mens est erigenda ad Deum.* This sentence, in precisely this form (though with *Dominum* for *Deum*) appears in Jerome, *Epistola* 58.6 to Paulinus; PL 22:583. It is then picked up, with trifling variants, by a number of later writers.

178. This last sentence, in exactly the same form in which it appears in the *Meditationes*, is found in Rabanus Maurus, *In Ecclesiasticum*, IV.5; PL

18. But you say: "I pray every day, yet I see no results from my prayers. As I came to them, so I leave them. Nobody answers me, nobody speaks to me, nobody gives me anything, and I seem to have labored in vain." So says human foolishness, paying no heed to what Truth itself promises, when it says, "Truly I say to you, whatsoever you ask in prayer, believe that you shall receive it, and it shall come to you."[179] Do not undervalue your prayer, therefore, for he to whom you pray does not undervalue it, but before it even comes out of your mouth, he himself orders it to be written down in his book. And there is not the least doubt that we should hope for one of two things: either that he will give us what we ask, or that he knows what will be more profitable for us.[180] So think of God in the best way you can, and of yourself in the worst way you can. You should believe in him more than you can think [of him]. Take all that time in which you are not thinking about God and reckon it to yourself as a loss. "All things are foreign to us: only time is our own."[181] So give yourself some free time, and wherever you may be, be yourself! Don't give yourself away to [outward] things: just lend yourself out [for a while]. So in whatever place you may be, cast your thought up to God,[182] and think of something for your soul's salvation.[183] For any place is suitable for meditation.

109:875A, who may have found it in a work by or attributed to Alcuin of York: see *Dicta beati Albini*; PL 100:567AB. It certainly predates the *Meditationes*, and also appears in the *De spiritu et anima* and *De interiori domo*.

179. Matt 21:22; Mark 11:24.

180. The section from the beginning of §18 to here is directly dependent on Bernard, *In Quadragesima, sermo* 5.5; SBOp 4:374–75.

181. L. Annaeus Seneca (Seneca the Younger), *Epistulae morales ad Lucilium, Ep.* I.1.4.

182. *Cogitationes tuas jacta in Deum*. This is the Old Latin version of Ps 54:23, which *ps.*-Bernard might have found in Hilary of Poitiers, Ambrose, Jerome, or a number of other patristic writers.

183. See Ps 118:81.

19. And so, gathering together all your mental faculties,[184] live freely with yourself, and, walking about in the breadth of your heart,[185] prepare there a splendid upper banqueting-room for Christ.[186] For the mind of a wise person is always with God. We should always have him before our eyes,[187] through whom we are, we know, and we are wise.[188] We have him as our Maker that we might exist; we should have him as our teacher that we may be wise; and so that we might be blessed, [we have him as] the bestower of inward sweetness.[189] And by this we know that his image—[the image], that is, of that supreme Trinity—is within ourselves. For just as he is, and is wise, and is good, so we, in our own small way, also exist, and know that we exist, and love that existence and knowledge.[190]

Use yourself, therefore, as God's temple,[191] because what is in you is like God, and the greatest honor [we can do] to God is to worship him and imitate him. You imitate him if you are devout, for a devout mind is a temple holy to God, and the heart is his best altar.[192] You worship him if you are merciful, just as he is merciful to all,[193] for to do good to all for the sake of God is an acceptable

---

184. *Tota ergo facultate animum colligens.* This is the sole appearance of the word *animus* (as distinct from *anima*) in the *Meditationes.*

185. Prov 7:3 according to the Septuagint, which the author could have found in Hilary of Poitiers, Ambrose, Bede, or Rabanus Maurus.

186. See Luke 22:12.

187. See Ps 15:8.

188. See Acts 17:28, but *ps.*-Bernard is now following Augustine.

189. This sentence is taken directly from Augustine, *De civitate Dei,* XI.25; PL 41:339.

190. For these last two sentences, see Augustine, *De Trinitate,* XV.xx.38; PL 42:1088.

191. See 1 Cor 3:16.

192. The last part of this sentence, in a slightly different form, is attributed to the third-century Pope Sixtus II: "A devout mind is a temple holy to God, and the best altar is a clean and sinless heart" (see PL 21:198A and PL 48:606A), but *ps.*-Bernard has taken it from Augustine, *De natura et gratia,* lxiv.77; PL 44:285.

193. Sir 2:13.

sacrifice to God.[194] Do everything as a child of God, so that you may be worthy of him who deigned to call you his child.[195]

But know that God is present in everything you do! Take care, then, lest your eyes or your thoughts linger on that which delights in wickedness. Do not say or do anything that is not right, even though you may enjoy it, and do not offend God by any act or gesture, him who, being present everywhere, sees whatever you do.[196] You therefore need to take the greatest care, for you live in the sight of a judge who sees everything. Yet for all that, you are always safe with him if you so prepare yourself that he may deign to be with you. If he is not with you by grace, he is with you by vengeance[197]—and woe to you if he is with you thus! Yet worse for you if he is not with you in this way! For God is truly angry with that sinner whom he does not scourge for his sins,[198] for whomever he does not correct here by scourging, he condemns hereafter.

194. See 1 Pet 2:5.

195. See John 1:12; Rom 8:16; 2 Cor 6:18; Gal 3:26.

196. These last two sentences are dependent on Augustine, *De civitate Dei*, XXII.23; PL 41:787.

197. *Si tecum non esse per gratiam, adest per vindictam.* This is a direct quotation from Gregory the Great, *In Ezechielem, I, hom.* 8.16; PL 76:860C.

198. This first part of the sentence is a direct quotation from Augustine, *Enarratio in Ps.* 98.11; PL 37:1266.

CHAPTER SEVEN

On Guarding the Heart and Zeal in Prayer

20. One thing is certain: death threatens you everywhere. The devil lies in wait to seize your soul when it leaves the body. But don't be afraid, for God, who dwells in you (if indeed he does dwell in you), will snatch you away from both death and the devil! For he is a faithful friend who will not forsake those who hope in him, unless he himself be first forsaken. He is forsaken when the heart, by means of a wandering mind, runs hither and thither among wicked and useless thoughts. It follows, then, that you should guard and control your heart with all care and watchfulness so that God can rest therein. For of all created things under the sun that are taken up with the vanities of the world,[199] there is nothing to be found that is more exalted, nothing more noble, nothing more like God than the human heart. This is why he seeks nothing from you except your heart. Cleanse it, therefore, by a complete confession[200] and continual prayer so that with a pure heart you may see God[201] by continual and careful consideration of God.[202] In every place be subject to him and attentive to him, and so adjust

199. See Eccl 1:14.
200. *Per puram confessionem*: see n. 139 above.
201. Matt 5:8.
202. Sir 14:22.

your way of life that you may be at peace within yourself. Love all people, and show yourself worthy to be loved by all, so that you may be a peacemaker,[203] and a child of God.[204] Thus you will be a good monk,[205] holy, humble, and upright, and when you are so, remember me.

21. Woe to me who say these things but do not do them! Or, if I sometimes do them, I don't persevere for long. I have them in my memory, but I don't put them into practice in my life. I talk about them, but I don't do them.[206] I ponder your law all day[207] in my heart and my mouth, yet what I do is contrary to the law. In it I read all about leading a godly life,[208] but I love reading rather than praying! Yet the only thing that divine Scripture teaches me is to love godliness, to preserve unity,[209] and to have charity.[210] But I, miserable wretch that I am, run more quickly to reading than to praying. I'd rather read than hear Masses. If someone comes looking for me, wanting to discuss their problems with me, I pick up some book that a number of others would like to have. I read in it and, by reading, lose the rewards of charity, the feeling of devotion, the tears of compunction, the profit of Masses, and the contemplation of heavenly things. And yet nothing in this life appears sweeter, nothing grasped more eagerly, nothing that so separates the mind from the love of the world, nothing that so strengthens the soul against temptations, nothing that so stirs up someone and helps him in every good deed and every labor as the grace of contemplation.

203. Matt 5:9.

204. See n. 194 above.

205. The author uses the term *monachus*.

206. The section from the beginning of this paragraph to here is paralleled in *De spiritu et anima*, 62; PL 40:827, and the last two sentences are taken directly from Augustine, *In Joannis evangelium, tract.* 75.5; PL 35:1830.

207. See Ps 1:2.

208. *Lego de religione*: see n. 168 above.

209. Eph 4:3.

210. See 1 Cor 13:1-3.

CHAPTER EIGHT

On the Hatred of Carelessness or Negligence in Prayer

22. Have mercy on me, O God,[211] for I sin more here where I ought to correct my sins. Often, when I pray in the monastery, I don't pay attention to what I say. I certainly pray with my mouth, but with my mind wandering far away I get no profit from my prayers. I am inside my body but outside my heart, and therefore I lose what I say. There is little to be gained from singing [praises] with the voice alone without the heart being involved as well. It is therefore great perversity—great stupidity indeed!—to presume to speak to the Lord of Majesty[212] in prayer while foolishly turning our ears away and turning our heart towards I know not what sort of nonsense. It is also complete madness, and something that deserves to be severely punished, when the vilest dust refuses to listen to the Creator of the Universe speaking to him! But how indescribably condescending is the Divine Goodness when, each day, it sees us unhappy wretches turning away our ears and hardening our hearts,[213] and nevertheless cries out to us,[214] saying,

211. Ps 50:3.

212. See Ps 28:3.

213. Ps 94:8.

214. The section from "It is therefore great perversity" to here is taken directly from Bernard, *De diversis, sermo* 23.6; SBOp 6/1:182, but Bernard himself now quotes Song 6:12 and not, as here, Isa 46:8.

"Return to the heart, you transgressors![215] Be still, and see that I am God!"[216]

God speaks to me in the psalm, and I to him; yet when I say the psalm, I pay no attention to whose psalm it is. I thus do a great injury to God when I pray to him to hear my prayer while I who pour it forth do not hear it! I beg him to pay heed to me while I pay no heed either to myself or to him. But what is even worse, by pondering on unclean and useless things in my heart, I raise up a horrible stench in his sight.

215. Isa 46:8.
216. Ps 45:11.

CHAPTER NINE

On the Unstable Nature of the Human Heart

23.[217] There is nothing in me more fickle than my heart. As often as it leaves my control and wanders off among evil thoughts, so often does it offend God.[218] My heart is an empty heart, unruly and unstable. While it is led by its own will and lacks divine guidance, it cannot stand firm in itself. It is more inconstant than inconstancy itself, distracted by an infinite number of things, and it runs to and fro, here and there, among countless preoccupations. Though it seeks rest in a multitude of things, it does not find it, but remains miserable in its quest and finds no repose. It does not agree with itself and is at odds with itself. It recoils from itself, altering its intentions, changing its mind, building up new plans, pulling down old ones, rebuilding what it has pulled down, changing and reorganizing the same thing again and again, now this way, now that, for it wants to do something and doesn't want to,[219] and it never stays

217. Certain passages in §§23–24 also appear in the *De spiritu et anima*: see Bultot, "Les 'Meditationes,'" 271.

218. These first two sentences are taken from Gregory the Great, *Regulae pastoralis*, III.14; PL 77:72AB.

219. Prov 13:4.

the same. It is like a swiftly turning mill[220] that refuses nothing but simply grinds up whatever is put in it. But if nothing is put in it, it wears itself out. In just the same way, my heart is always on the move and never at rest. Whether I'm asleep or awake, it dreams or thinks about whatever happens to come its way.

If you throw sand into a mill, it will reject it, pitch will pollute it, chaff will cause it to seize up. In just the same way, gloomy thoughts trouble my heart, unclean thoughts defile it, empty thoughts disturb and weary it. Thus, if my heart does not concern itself with future joy or seek divine help, it is separated from the love of heavenly things and given over to the love of worldly things. But when it slips away from the former and immerses itself in the latter, vanity receives it, useless curiosity[221] leads it, desire entices it, pleasure seduces it, lust pollutes it, envy torments it, anger disturbs it, and sorrow afflicts it. Thus, in all these wretched ways, it is plunged into all manner of vices, for it has forsaken the one and only God, who could have satisfied it.

24. It busies itself with a multitude of matters and looks here and there for a place where it can rest, but it finds nothing to satisfy it, unless it returns to him [who made it].[222] It is led from thought to thought and changes continually with changing feelings and occupations: it tries, at the very least, to fill itself up with the variety of all these things, even though they are of such a nature that

220. This likening of the heart to a swiftly turning mill appears to have been inspired by John Cassian, *Collationes*, 1.18; PL 49:507C–8B.

221. *Curiositas* does not mean "curious" in the usual modern sense, but refers to things that titillate and pander to our human curiosity, and *curiositas* was roundly condemned by a multitude of monastic writers, including Bernard, as being both useless and dangerous. See Richard Newhauser, "The Sin of Curiosity and the Cistercians," in *Erudition at God's Service: Studies in Medieval Cistercian History, XI*, ed. John R. Sommerfeldt, CS 98 (Kalamazoo, MI: Cistercian Publications, 1987), 71–95.

222. See Augustine, *Confessiones*, I.i.1; PL 32:661.

they cannot satisfy it.[223] Thus, when divine grace is withdrawn, the heart becomes ever more wretched.

When it returns to itself and examines what it has thought it finds nothing, because it did no work there. There was only a worthless thought that makes much out of nothing. Thus at last the imagination, deluded by demons, deceives us. [How?] [First,] God commands me to offer him my heart,[224] but because I am not obedient or subject to the God who commands this, I am in rebellion and opposition to myself. Thus, since I cannot be subject to myself until I have made myself subject to him, I, who do not wish to serve God willingly, serve myself unwillingly! As a result, my heart invents more things in a single moment than the whole human race could accomplish in a whole year! Since I am not united with God, I am divided in myself. But the only way in which I can be united with him is by charity, [the only way I can be] subject to him is by humility, and [the only way I can be] truly humble is by truth.

25. What I need to do, therefore, is to examine myself truthfully and know how lowly, how frail, and how inconstant I am. Then, when I know my utter wretchedness, I need to cleave to him by whom I am, and without whom I am nothing and can do nothing. But since I withdrew from God by sinning, the only way I can return to him is by making a true[225] confession. I will confess,[226] then, all that must be confessed, for I have never confessed[227] my sins in the exact way and with the exact intention with which I sinned. Nor did I remember them all, either because I committed them so long ago or because there were so many of them. And if

223. The section from "for it has forsaken the one and only God" to here has been taken from Odo of Cluny, *Collationes*, I.6; PL 133:524AB, with the usual mixture of direct quotation and paraphrase.

224. See Prov 23:26.

225. This time, the author uses *vera*, not *pura*: see n. 139 above.

226. The verb here is *fateor*, not the more usual *confiteor*.

227. He now uses *confessus*, from *confiteor*. There is no difference between the two verbs.

I did confess then, I did not do so fully and sincerely, because I was ashamed of them. In addition to that, I split up my confession, revealing different things to different priests, and thus, by making my confession in bits and pieces, I failed to receive the forgiveness on which I had counted. For it is a detestable pretense to split up your sin and merely scratch its surface instead of completely tearing it out by the roots. Confession is useless unless it is made with a truthful tongue and a pure heart.[228] And in order for three to bear witness to us in heaven, the Father, Son, and Holy Spirit,[229] let us add the witness of the priest to that of our heart and our mouth, so that "in the mouth of two or three witnesses every word shall stand."[230]

26.[231] "But," you say, "it is enough for me to confess to God alone, for without him a priest cannot absolve me from sins." To this it is not I but blessed James who replies, saying, "Confess your sins to one another."[232] For it is entirely appropriate that we who have so defied God by sinning should humble ourselves before his priests and ministers by repenting, so that we who did not lack a [divine] Mediator to preserve grace cannot now recover it save through a human mediator.

Let us therefore sigh and lament, and be in the greatest fear and dread for our sins. Let us run around anxiously, looking for those who may help us or intercede for us. Let us, who would not stand humbly before our Creator, bow down humbly before a mortal man. For there is nothing more beneficial than this: that we

228. The author's discussion of the nature and need for "true" or "pure" confession has been influenced by Bernard, *In assumptione B.V.M., sermo* 2.5; SBOp 5:235.

229. See 1 John 5:7.

230. Matt 18:16; 2 Cor 13:1.

231. The whole of §26 is taken from Hugh of Saint-Victor, *De sacramentis christianae fidei*, II.xiv.8; PL 176:564D–69B. There is much omission, but a considerable amount of direct quotation. See also *ps.*-Augustine, *De visitatione infirmorum*, II.4 "Quod non sufficiat soli Deo confiteri"; PL 40:1154–55.

232. Jas 5:16.

should repent in our heart and confess our faults with our mouth until God, who is mercifully present to us by grace, should goad our heart to repentance. May he then be so present to us that he will grant forgiveness of sins to those who confess them.

But should it so happen that a sinner is truly penitent, but that some unforeseen need arises that prevents him from coming to confession, we should firmly believe that the great High Priest fulfills in him what a mortal [priest] could not do. In this case, what this person wished to do but was not able to accomplish is considered by God as having been done, since he did not reject confession because he scorned it, but was prevented from going by [unavoidable] necessity.

On the Dislike of Being Corrected, and of Being Accused of One's Failures and Faults

27. In the Chapter Room,[233] where I ought to have corrected my sins, I added to them. When I have been accused of them, I made some sort of excuse for them or denied them altogether. Or, what's worse, I defended them, and replied impatiently that there is no sin with which I am not stained or can be stained! [But since this is true,] it is just that I should put all excuses to one side and promise amendment from wherever and by whomever I am accused, so that I may be delivered from the sin I have committed or am about to commit.

Being so terrified of the multitude of my own iniquities, I have been afraid to reprove the transgressions of others, and thus I have become one who brings death, for I have not expelled the poison that I could have expelled by speaking out. I have been angry with others who have reproved me for my own faults and have hated those whom I ought to have loved. I wished that all those things that either hurt me or displeased me had never existed, even though I knew that they were good in themselves and made by a

---

233. *In capitulo.* In this section, the writer is speaking of the Chapter of Faults that we discussed in chap. 4 of part one.

good Maker. The reason they hurt me, therefore, was that I was evil and used them in an evil way, for the only thing at enmity with me is myself! So whatever can hurt me is here with me, and I am myself my own burden.[234]

28. I even wished that God would not know of my sins, or would be unwilling or unable to punish them. In other words, I wanted God to be unwise, unjust, and powerless, though if he were, he would not be God. There is no pride greater than my pride, and therefore "the words of my sins are far from my salvation."[235] All pride, then, is distrusted by God and hateful to him, and it cannot ever find favor in his eyes. [God and pride] dwell in different lodgings, and just as they cannot live together in heaven, so they cannot live together in the same soul. [The soul] was born in heaven, but being, as it were, unmindful of the way in which it fell from there, it has not been able to return there afterwards.[236]

When the weather has turned to rain, or when it has been too cold or too hot, I have murmured unjustly against God. For everything that we have received to be used for living, we have turned to the use of wickedness.[237] It is only just, therefore, that we who have sinned in everything should be punished in everything.[238] At the Sacred Mystery [of the Mass] I have often sung falsetto[239] so as

234. See Luke 11:46.

235. Ps 21:2.

236. The section from "All pride, then is distrusted by God" to here is taken directly from Hildebert of Lavardin, *Epistola* I.21 to Athalisa; PL 171:196D.

237. This sentence is taken from Gregory the Great, *In evangelia, hom.* 35.1; PL 76:1260AB.

238. See Odo of Cluny, *Collationes*, I.8; PL 133:525C. *Ps.*-Bernard changes Odo's *deliquimus* to *peccavimus*.

239. *Vocem meam fregi*, which means literally "I have broken my voice," but there can be no doubt that the writer is referring to that falsetto singing that was specifically prohibited in the earliest Institutes of the Cistercian General Chapter: "Men ought to sing with manly voices and not imitate the lasciviousness of actors by singing with shrill voices [*tinnulis*] like women or with what are commonly called falsetto voices." See *Instituta Generalis Capituli* 75; Chrysogonus Waddell, *Narrative and Legislative Texts from Early Cîteaux. Latin Text in Dual*

to chant more sweetly, taking greater delight in the sound of the voice than in compunction of heart. But God, from whom nothing that is done unlawfully can be hidden,[240] seeks a pure heart, not a melodious voice. For while the singer pleases the people with his notes, he provokes God with his wicked ways. I have often extorted from my superiors [in the monastery] permission to speak[241] or do something by pestering them too much or being too cunning, not paying heed—miserable wretch that I am!—that we only deceive ourselves if, secretly or openly, we persuade our spiritual father[242] to order us to do something that we ourselves actually desire to do!

29. There have been many times when I really wanted a needle or a little knife[243] or something equally useful but did not confess it. It was such a trifling matter that I did not think it a sin. But there is not much difference between wanting something of little value or of great value, since the yearning for either is equally sinful. It's not the little knife that's at fault, but the desire for the knife; nor is gold at fault, but the lust for gold.[244] When I was at work, I did not work as hard as I should, nor, indeed, as hard as I could. In silence, too, I have been idle, which is the greatest sin.[245] For in silence no one should be idle, so that in his idleness he does not think of how he might be useful to his neighbor. But neither should he be so busy that he does not seek the contemplation of God.[246] For it is little profit to us if we do not help others when we can.

Edition with English Translation and Notes, Studia et Documenta, IX (Brecht: *Cîteaux—Commentarii cistercienses*, 1999), 360, 489.

240. See Heb 4:13.

241. See RSB 6: "if permission to speak is granted at all, it should only be granted very rarely."

242. For the novices in the monastery, the *pater spiritualis* was the novice master; for the professed monks, the abbot.

243. This is a reference to RSB 55.19.

244. See 1 Tim 6:10.

245. See RSB 48.1.

246. These last two sentences are taken directly from Augustine, *De civitate Dei*, XIX.19; PL 41:647.

I have often boasted of my faults, thinking that by doing so I was showing how strong I was, whereas I was actually falling into sin. I have even made vices of virtues. When justice exceeds its bounds, it produces the vice of cruelty, and too much devotion does away with discipline. Thus it often happens that a vice is accounted a virtue. Self-indulgent sloth[, for example,] is taken to be meekness, and the vice of laziness masquerades as the virtue of [meditative] repose.[247] I pretended to be what I was not: I said that I wanted what I didn't want, and didn't want what I wanted. I said one thing with my mouth and planned quite another in my heart, and thus, under the skin of a sheep, I retained the morality of a fox.[248] And what is the morality of a fox but a lukewarm monastic life,[249] worldly thoughts, counterfeit confession, short and rare compunction, obedience without devotion, prayer without intention, reading without edification, speaking without thinking.[250]

30. Oh, these things are so hard for me to say, for saying them really hurts me. But because I do not deny that I am a sinner and because I acknowledge my sin, perhaps this very acknowledgement of my faults before God, the merciful Judge, will procure my forgiveness.[251] I will tell him, then, I will tell him of my wretchedness, so that his mercy may perhaps move him [to forgive me]. I will tell him of my sin, for "the recognition of sin is the beginning

247. These last three sentences, illustrating how vices can be mistaken for virtues, are taken directly from Isidore of Seville, *Sententiae*, II.34.4 and II.35.3; PL 83:635D, 636D.

248. See Matt 7:15, though there it is wolves, not foxes, that are in sheep's clothing.

249. *Tepida conversatio*, where *conversatio* does not mean conversation, but behavior, conduct, or the monastic life.

250. Except for the *ficta confessio*, all these problems have been taken directly from Bernard, *In ascensione Domini, sermo* 6.7; SBOp 5:154.

251. These first two sentences are taken directly from Gregory the Great, *In Ezechielem, I, hom.* 11.5; PL 76:907CD. The first sentence, but not the second, also appears in Odo of Cluny, *Collationes*, III.6; PL 133:594A, who has taken it from Gregory.

of salvation."[252] I have a large tonsure and wear a cowl,[253] I keep the rules of fasting, I sing [in choir] at the required hours,[254] but my heart is far from my God! When I look at myself outwardly, just on the surface, all seems to be well, and I do not feel the worm inside me that gnaws away at what is within. This is why Hosea says, "Strangers have devoured my strength, and I did not know it."[255] And so, being wholly given over to the pursuit of what is outside me, and not knowing what is inside me, I was poured out like water[256] and reduced to nothing,[257] forgetting the past, neglecting the present, and making no provision for the future. I am ungrateful for favors, prone to do evil, and slow to do good.

252. L. Annaeus Seneca (Seneca the Younger), *Episulae morales ad Lucilium, Ep.* I.28.9, quoting Epicurus: see *Epicurea*, ed. Hermann Usener (Leipzig: Teubner, 1887), 318 (fragment 522). I very much doubt that *ps.*-Bernard had been reading Seneca, much less Epicurus. The *dictum* was well known and is quoted by Bernard, *De diversis, sermo* 40.3; SBOp 6/1:237.

253. I presume that this is what the writer means, though the Latin is odd. What he says is that he wears a *vestem rotundam*, a round or circular garment, an expression I have never seen elsewhere. Bernard himself simply says *vestis necdum mutata est*, "the [monastic] garment has not yet been put off." *Rotundus* can also mean well fitting or elegant, and Antony Batt, in his *A Hive of Sacred Honie-Combes*, 43, translates it as "a comely platted garment." I have grave doubts about that, and my own view is that the author is referring to the cowl—*cuculla* or *cucullus*—prescribed in RSB 55 as one of the items with which a monk must be provided, the others being two tunics, a scapular for work, stockings, and shoes. I would suggest that conclusive proof for this may be found in the passage parallel to this that appears in the *De interiori domo*, 38; PL 184:528A, where the writer says that he has a *magna corona et ampla cuculla*, "a large tonsure and voluminous cowl." The cowl was the distinguishing feature of a monk, as may be seen from the well-known proverb, *cucullus non facit monachum*, "the cowl does not make the monk." So what the writer is saying is that with his monastic tonsure and cowl, he looks exactly as a monk should, but—alas!—he does not behave like one.

254. I.e., the seven daily Offices of Lauds, Prime, Terce, Sext, Nones, Vespers, and Compline and the Night Office.

255. Hos 7:9.

256. Ps 21:15.

257. Ps 72:22.

31. If I do not examine myself, I do not know myself; but if I do examine myself, I cannot stand myself! I find so many things within me that need to be corrected and of which I am ashamed, and the more often and the more minutely I examine myself, the more abominations I find in the corners of my heart.[258] For ever since I began to sin, I could not let a single day go by without sinning, and I still do not stop sinning, but from day to day add sins to sins. I examine what is right there before my eyes, and I do not lament. I see things that should make me blush, but I do not blush. I look at things over which I should grieve, but I do not grieve. This is a token of death and a mark of damnation. For a bodily member that feels no pain is dead, and you cannot cure a disease that you do not know you have. I am capricious and careless, and instead of correcting myself I return each day to the sins I have confessed. Nor do I pay any heed to the pit into which I, miserable wretch, have fallen,[259] or into which I have made or seen others fall. And when I ought to weep and pray for the evil things I have done and the good things I have failed to do, then— alas!—I have done just the opposite. Instead of being fervent in prayer, I have become lukewarm and cold, and now remain cold and unfeeling. I cannot therefore weep for myself, for the gift of tears[260] has been taken from me.

258. This first section, from the beginning of §31 to here, is based on Anselm of Canterbury, *Oratio* 52; PL 158:970C–71A.

259. Prov 26:27.

260. *Gratia lacrymarum*: see n. 146 above.

CHAPTER ELEVEN

On Conscience, Which Accompanies Us Everywhere and Continually Goads Us

32. I cannot hide my sins, for wherever I go my conscience is with me, carrying with it whatever I have put there, whether good or evil. It keeps safe everything that has been entrusted to it while I am alive, and it will give it back to me when I am dead. If I do evil, it is there, and if I seem to have done well, and have been praised for it, it is there. It is there while I am alive; it follows me in death. Whether to my glory or my detriment, wherever I am it is inseparable from me in accordance with the nature of what is entrusted to it.[261] Thus, in my own house and from my own family[262] I have accusers, witnesses, judges, and torturers. My conscience accuses me, memory is its witness, reason the judge, pleasure the prison, fear the torturer, and [worldly] delights the torment. For as many as were the evil delights, so many will be the terrible torments in punishment. For as we are delighted, thus are we punished.

261. The section from the beginning of §32 to here has been taken directly from Bernard, *Epistola 42 de moribus et officio espiscoporum*, 6.21; SBOp 7:116–17.

262. I.e., from my own body.

CHAPTER TWELVE

Of the Three Enemies of Humankind: The Flesh, the World, and the Devil[263]

33. Help me, O Lord my God, for my enemies have surrounded my soul:[264] the body, that is, the world, and the devil. From the body I cannot flee, nor can it flee from me. I have to carry it around because it is tied to me. It is not lawful to kill it; I am forced to sustain it. And when I indulge it, I am nourishing my enemy against myself! For if I feed it enough and make it strong, its health and strength fight against me.

As to the world, it surrounds me and besieges me on all sides, and through five gates—namely, the five bodily senses of sight, hearing, taste, smell, and touch—it wounds me with its arrows; through these five windows death enters my soul. The eye looks, and diverts the mind's attention. The ear hears, and turns aside the intention of the heart. Smelling hinders thinking. The mouth speaks and deceives. By touching, the fire of lust is stirred up at

263. Chapters twelve and thirteen are heavily dependent on Bernard, *Dominica VI post Pentecosten, sermo* 3.4–5; PL 183:343A–44A (not in SBOp) (see Bultot, "Les 'Meditationes,'" 261–66), and also on Bernard's *In Cantica, sermo* 85.ii.4–6; SBOp 2:309–11. The idea of the world, the flesh, and the devil as the three enemies of the soul goes back to the earliest days of Christianity.

264. Ps 16:9.

every trifling opportunity, and unless it is put out straightaway, it will suddenly take over the whole body, setting it on fire and burning it up. First it titillates the flesh a little with [lustful] thoughts. Then it pollutes the mind with [ideas of] shameful delights; and at last, by giving its consent to this depravity, it subjugates the mind to itself.

Now with regard to the devil, whom I cannot see and of whom, therefore, I am less wary, he has drawn his bow and has his arrows ready to wound me unexpectedly.[265] He has talked of hiding his snares and has said, "Who shall see them?"[266] He has laid a snare in gold and silver and in all those things that we misuse when we wickedly delight in them and are thereby ensnared by them. But not only has he laid a snare; he has also put down sticky birdlime.[267] Birdlime is the love of possessions, the enjoyment of close relationships, a desire for honor, and the pleasures of the flesh. By these the soul is glued down and netted, so that it cannot fly though the highways of the heavenly Zion[268] on the wings of contemplation. The devil's arrows are anger, envy, lust, and other similar things by which the soul is wounded. And who is there who can extinguish his fiery darts?

> Alas! a faithful [soul] is often vanquished by these weapons.
> Woe to me! How many [foes] do I see, ready to make war
> against me?[269]

265. See Ps 10:3.

266. Ps 63:6.

267. Birdlime is an adhesive substance used for trapping birds. It is smeared over a branch or twig, and when a small bird lands on the branch its feet stick to it so that it can then easily be caught.

268. See Bernard, *De diversis, sermo* 23.3; SBOp 6/1:176.

269. *Proh dolor! his telis superatur saepe fidelis. / Heu mihi! quot video bella parata mihi?* The first part of this distich is from Hildebert of Lavardin, *Vita b. Mariae Aegyptiacae*, I; PL 171:1323D; Walther, *Initia*, 18159. The second part appears in a variant form—*Bella mihi video, bella paratur, ait*—in Matthew of Vendôme, *Carmina*, PL 205:984D; Walther, *Initia*, 17437. But in that passage

34. Arrows fly about on every side. Everywhere there are trials, everywhere dangers. Wherever I turn, I find no safety. I am afraid of everything, both things that please me and things that sadden or trouble me. Being hungry and eating, sleeping and waking, working and resting all fight against me.[270] I am as suspicious of making a joke as I am of being angry, for there are many whom I have offended by jesting. I am just as afraid of good fortune as I am of adversity, for good fortune is so agreeable that it makes me careless and deceives me. Adversity, on the other hand, has something bitter about it, and it makes me as distrustful and fearful as do bitter drinks. I am more afraid of the wicked things I do in secret than of those I do openly. The wickedness that nobody sees, nobody reproves, and if we have no fear of anyone reproving us, the Tempter is safe in attacking us and evil is committed more easily.[271]

It is clear that in both cases there is war, in both cases there is danger, in both cases there are things to be feared, and just like someone passing through enemy territory, we must keep a careful watch on all sides and check out any threat.[272] The flesh suggests soft and pleasant things to me, the world vain things, the devil bitter things. For as often as fleshly thoughts doggedly disturb my mind [with ideas] of food and drink, or sleep, or some other such thing pertaining to the care of the flesh, it is the flesh speaking to me. When vain and empty thoughts lodge in my heart about worldly ambition, ostentation, or self-importance, they come from

----

from Bernard on which the writer is here dependent, Bernard writes *Heu me! Domine Deus, quia undique mihi bella* . . . .

270. From the beginning of §34 to here (and possibly from the second line of the distich), the writer is following *ps.*-Bernard, *In Quadragesima, sermo* 6.3; PL 183:182C (not in SBOp).

271. This last sentence has been taken directly from Bernard, *Ep.* 115.1 to Alia; SBOp 7:294. The whole of the next paragraph, to the end of §34, is entirely dependent on Bernard, *De diversis, sermo* 23.3; SBOp 6/1:180. As usual, some of it is quoted directly, some of it is abbreviated, and there are some additions.

272. Lit. "keep turning our neck [to look]."

the world. But when I am provoked to wrath and anger and bitterness of soul, these are the devil's suggestions, and these we should resist just as if we were resisting the devil himself, and keep ourselves safe from them just as if we were keeping ourselves safe from damnation itself. It is the business of demons to implant evil suggestions; our business is not to consent to them. For as often as we resist, we conquer the devil, we delight the angels, and we honor God. For he himself encourages us to fight, helps us to be victorious, watches us striving in the combat, raises us up when we fall, and crowns us when we conquer.

CHAPTER THIRTEEN

On the Attacks of These Three Aforesaid Enemies

35. My flesh is from dirt,[273] and from it, therefore, I have dirty and sensuous thoughts. From the world I have vain and prying thoughts, and from the devil evil and malicious thoughts. These three enemies attack me and pursue me, now openly, now secretly, but always maliciously. The devil trusts more in the help of the flesh because an enemy from one's own household does more harm.[274] [The flesh] has made an alliance with him for my destruction, inasmuch as it was born in sin[275] and nourished in sin, corrupted by vice from its very beginning, but tainted to a much greater degree by its evil habits. This is why the flesh lusts against the spirit,[276] why it continually murmurs and has no time for discipline, why it suggests unlawful things, fails to obey reason, and is not curbed by any fear. That slithering serpent, that enemy of

273. Job 33:6. *Lutum* means clay, mire, dirt, loam, slime, and so on. Here it is best translated as *dirt* so as to lead to the dirty (*lutosas*) thoughts.

274. The first part of §35 to this point is dependent on Bernard, *Dominica VI post Pentecosten, sermo* 3.5; PL 183:343D–44A (not in SBOp). All that follows, from here to the end of §35, is taken directly from Bernard, *In Quadragesima, sermo* 5.1–3; SBOp 4:372–73, with considerable omissions and a few additions.

275. Ps 50:7.

276. Gal 5:17.

the human race, comes to the flesh and helps it and uses it. For he has no other desire, no other business, no other purpose than to destroy our souls.

He it is who constantly plans wickedness, speaks subtly, suggests things skillfully, and deceives cunningly. He breathes into us unlawful ideas, he enflames us with poisonous thoughts, he instigates wars, he nourishes hatred, he incites gluttony, he stirs up lust, he arouses the desires of the flesh, he prepares opportunities for sin, and he never ceases from battering at the human heart in a thousand harmful ways. This is how he strikes us with our own staff and binds our hands with our own belt, so that the flesh, which was given us to be our helper, becomes for us a stumbling-block and our downfall. It is a hard struggle and a grave danger to fight against an enemy from our own household, especially when we are strangers and he lives there. He is on his own ground; we are exiles and pilgrims. There is also great danger in fighting frequently—indeed, continually—against the devil's deceitful wiles, for his subtle nature and long practice in malice have made him very cunning.

CHAPTER FOURTEEN

On the Desire for Our Heavenly Homeland and on Its Supreme Happiness[277]

36. Deliver me from my enemies, O my God, and from those who hate me, for they are too strong for me.[278] Until today I have lived opposed to myself; let me now, by your grace, begin to live for myself. For we should live in this world in such a way that when the body begins to be devoured by worms in the tomb, the soul may rejoice with the saints in heaven.[279] That is the goal to which the spirit must be directed, to which it is to go. That is the goal to which we should hasten, where we shall live forever, and where we shall no longer have any fear of death. If we love this fleeting and transitory life where we live with so much toil and where we scarcely satisfy our bodily needs with eating, drinking, and sleeping, how much more ought we to love that eternal life, where we know no toil, where there is always the greatest delight,

277. After the first five sentences, the rest of this chapter—i.e. the rest of §36 and the whole of §37—is taken directly from *ps.*-Augustine, *De rectitudine catholicae conversationis*, 22; PL 40:1184. There is the usual mix of direct quotation, paraphrase, and omissions, as well as a few minor additions.

278. See Ps 17:18; 58:2; 142:9.

279. See *ps.*-Augustine, *De veteri et novo testamenti, sermo* 104.7; PL 39:1948.

the highest happiness, happy freedom and happy blessedness, where we shall be like the angels of God,[280] and where the righteous shall shine like the sun in the kingdom of their Father.[281] If the light of their bodies will be as bright as the sun, can you imagine how bright their souls will be? There will be no sadness there, no distress, no sorrow, no fear, no toil, no death, but only eternal well-being that will last for ever and ever.

37. No malice arises there, and there is no bodily misery, no sickness, nor any want at all. There is no hunger there, no thirst, no cold, no heat, no weakness that comes from fasting, no temptations by the Enemy, no will to sin, nor any capacity to do wrong: there is only the fullness of joy and delight. Since humans are now the companions of the angels, they will forever remain untroubled by any bodily infirmity. There, there will be infinite delight and eternal blessedness, and once we have been received into that [blessedness], we will be kept there forever. There, there is rest from our labors,[282] peace from enemies, pleasure from what is new,[283] safety for eternity, and sweetness and delight in the vision of God. No one there can be called a pilgrim, for whoever is worthy to come there will remain safe and secure in their own homeland, ever joyful and ever satisfied with the vision of God. The more we are obedient to God here [on earth], so much the greater shall be the reward we shall receive from him there, and the more we love God, the more closely shall we see him whom we long to behold.

280. Matt 22:30.

281. Matt 13:43.

282. See Matt 11:28.

283. *Amoenitas de novitate*. This may seem odd until we remember that it is an allusion to 1 Tim 6:20: *O Timothee, depositum custodi, devitans profanas vocum novitates et oppositiones falsi nominis scientiae*. In other words, guard the deposit of the faith, do not venture beyond its bounds, and avoid the profane novelties invented by such heretics as Peter Abelard and so many others. *Novelties* were, by definition, dangerous and to be shunned, but in heaven *novitas* can actually give pleasure or delight.

CHAPTER FIFTEEN

On the Nature and Feelings of the Old Self,[284] and Its Mortification and Transformation through Christ

38. Our days are like a shadow on the earth, and there is no length to them.[285] Then, when we seem to stand firm, we are actually nothing.[286] Why, then, do people store up treasure on earth,[287] when all passes away in no time at all, both what is collected and those who collected it? And you, you men and women, what fruit do you expect from the world, whose fruit is ruin and whose end is death? How I wish you were wise and would understand, and make provision for your last days!

I know someone who lived with you as a member of the family for many years,[288] who sat at your table and accepted food from

---

284. *Veteris hominis*, the "old man" of Eph 4:22, which is being corrupted by deceitful desires. So far as I have been able to trace, this whole final chapter, §§39–40, is not (for once) taken from some patristic or medieval source, but is rather a catena of biblical quotations describing the nature of the *vetus homo* and the battle against it. There is one very brief quotation from Bernard right at the end.

285. 1 Chr 29:15. See also Ps 143:4.

286. See 1 Cor 10:12.

287. Matt 6:19.

288. I.e. the old self, *vetus homo*.

your hand, slept in your arms, and talked with you whenever he wanted. He is your servant by hereditary law.[289] But because you spoiled him from his earliest years and spared the rod,[290] he has become insolent. He has lifted up his heel over your head,[291] reduced you to servitude, and cruelly lords it over you.

39. But maybe you say, "Just who is this?" It is your old self, who tramples your spirit underfoot,[292] who sets at naught the desirable land,[293] who relishes only the things of the flesh. This old self was blind from birth,[294] and deaf, and dumb, grown old in evil days,[295] a rebel against virtue and truth, an enemy of the cross of Christ.[296] He ridicules the upright and those who walk simply,[297] but he himself walks among great and wonderful things above himself.[298] His arrogance is greater than his strength.[299] He respects no one. He says in his folly, "There is no God."[300] He withers away at the good deeds of others and feeds on their evil ones. He feeds on unclean thoughts, and in these he will not weary of sinning until the end.[301] He scatters and squanders his own property like

289. *Jure haereditario servus tuus est*: see Lev 24:44-46, which explains that the Israelites should take their servants, male and female, from the nations around them or from strangers in their midst, and not from their own people. The Israelites may then leave them to their descendants *haereditario jure*, by hereditary law or by right of inheritance. *Ps.*-Bernard is here referring to the alien *vetus homo* that we have inherited from Adam and Eve. He should be our servant but has become our master.

290. Prov 13:24.

291. Ps 40:9; John 13:18.

292. See Ps 55:2.

293. Ps 105:24.

294. John 9:1.

295. Dan 13:52.

296. Phil 3:18.

297. Prov 10:9.

298. Ps 130:1.

299. Isa 16:6.

300. Ps 52:1.

301. Sir 23:24.

a prodigal,[302] but covets and steals that of others like a miser. He accumulates for himself what is shameful and degrading, and by his hypocrisy and sly cunning he provokes the wrath of God.[303]

This old self is born wholly in sin, and is therefore brought up as a friend of iniquity, a child of death,[304] a vessel of wrath to be reproached, fit for destruction.[305] But although this is what he is like, "he explains the righteousness of God and takes his covenant into his mouth. He hates discipline and casts his Lord behind his back. When he sees a thief, he runs along with him, and he allies himself with adulterers. He sets out a stumbling-block for his mother's son."[306] On earth, he stores up wrath against the day of wrath.[307] He wants to take away your inheritance[308] and deprive you of your heavenly country,[309] yet you do not seek to avenge so great an injury, but ignore it! You do not speak a harsh word against him or show him an angry countenance, but smile when he deludes you! You play games with somebody who mocks you, but don't you know that it is Ishmael playing games with you?[310] This is not a child's game, simple and innocent. It is the soul's delusion, persecution, and death. He has already hurled you into the pit that he has made.[311] You are already weakened[312] and weighed down with the yoke of a wretched servitude,[313] miserably and meanly trampled under his feet.[314]

302. See Luke 15:13.

303. Job 36:13.

304. 1 Sam 20:30.

305. Rom 9:22.

306. Ps 49:16-20.

307. Rom 2:5.

308. This is an allusion to Jacob's seeking to deprive Esau of his inheritance: see Gen 25:29-34.

309. Tob 3:15.

310. See Gen 21:9: the reference is to the rivalry between Isaac and Ishmael.

311. Ps 7:16.

312. Or "emasculated" (*effeminatus*).

313. Gal 5:1.

314. Isa 28:3.

40. O wretched and miserable mortal! Who will deliver you from the bonds of this reproach?[315] Let God arise,[316] let this armed man fall! Let the enemy of humankind fall and be destroyed, he who despises God,[317] who worships himself, who loves the world, who serves the devil. What do you think? If you judge rightly you will say with me, "He is guilty of death,[318] let him be crucified!"[319] So don't pretend, don't delay, don't be merciful, but quickly, boldly, violently crucify the old self, but [do it] on the cross of Christ, in which there is life and salvation. If you call on him from your heart, your Crucified One will hear you and graciously reply, "Today you shall be with me in Paradise."[320]

Oh, the goodness of Christ! Oh, the unexpected salvation of a miserable wretch! How freely given and how sure is the love of God, how amazing his sweetness, how unexpected his favor, how unconquerable his clemency, so that if any cry out to him, he hears them, because he is merciful.[321] Oh, how great is the mercy of God! How indescribable the movement of the right hand of the Most High![322] Yesterday you were in darkness, today in the brightness of light.[323] Yesterday in a lion's mouth,[324] today in the hand of a Mediator. Yesterday at the gates of hell, today in the delights of Paradise.

But what use are all these words of advice if you do not blot out from the book of your conscience the words of death? What use are all these writings, read and understood, if you do not read and understand yourself? Pay close attention, then, to this inward

315. Tob 3:15.
316. Ps 67:2.
317. *Contemptor Dei*: a common expression among the Fathers.
318. Matt 26:66.
319. Matt 27:23.
320. Luke 23:43.
321. Sir 2:13.
322. Ps 76:11.
323. See Isa 9:2.
324. I.e., the devil's mouth: see 1 Pet 5:8.

reading, so that you may read, examine, and understand yourself. You should read to love God, to fight and conquer the world and every enemy. Thus your toil may be turned into rest, your sorrow into joy,[325] and after the darkness of this life you may see the first light of the dawning day,[326] and see, too, at midday the Sun of Righteousness,[327] in whom you will behold the Bridegroom with the bride, one and the same Lord of Glory,[328] who lives and reigns for endless ages. Amen.

325. John 16:20.

326. Job 3:9.

327. Mal 4:2.

328. 1 Cor 2:8, but the writer has taken this very last section to here, from "in whom you will behold," from Bernard, *In Cantica, sermo* 27.iv.7; SBOp 1:186.

Index of Classical, Patristic, and Medieval Sources

The numbers refer to the numbered footnotes to the translation.

[Anon.]

De interiori domo, xxviii.61 76

De spiritu et anima, 31 98

De spiritu et anima, 51 76, 143

De spiritu et anima, 52 9

De spiritu et anima, 55 115

De spiritu et anima, 62 206

Regula ad virgines, 16 139

Ambrose of Milan

De bono mortis, ii.6 53

Anselm of Canterbury 77

Oratio 52 258

Ps.-Anselm of Canterbury

*Meditatio super
    Miserere, 27* 65

Arnold of Bonneval

De operibus sex dierum 124

Augustine of Hippo

Confessiones, I.i.1 222

Contra Maximinum, II.ix.1 106

De civitate Dei, XI.25 189

De civitate Dei, XI.31 111

De civitate Dei, XIX.19 246

De civitate Dei, XX.14 50

De civitate Dei, XXII.23 196

De natura boni, 1 108

*De natura et gratia,
    lxiv.77* 192

De Trinitate, IV, proem. 145

De Trinitate, VIII.vii.11 3

De Trinitate, XIV.viii.11 22

De Trinitate, XIV.xii.15 23

De Trinitate, XV.xx.38 190

De Trinitate, XV.xxi.41 38

*Enarratio in Psalmos
    98.11* 198

Enarratio in Psalmos 145.5 4

*In Joannis evangelium,
    tract. 75.5* 206

*Quaestionum evangeliorum
    lib. 2, qu. 39* 34

Ps.-Augustine of Hippo

*De rectitudine catholicae
    conversationis, 21* 57

*De rectitudine catholicae
    conversationis, 22* 277

*De rectitudine catholicae
    conversationis, 23* 101

*De veteri et novo testamenti,
    sermo 104.7* 279

Formula honestae vitae   98
Manuale, 24   65, 159
Sermo 48 ad fratres in
    eremo commorantes   72
De visitatione infirmorum,
    II.4   231

Bede the Venerable
De die judicii   51, 52, 102

Benedict of Nursia
Regula S. Benedicti, 6   241
Regula S. Benedicti, 48.1   245
Regula S. Benedicti, 50   175
Regula S. Benedicti, 55.19   243

Bernard of Clairvaux
De diversis, sermo
    19.1   94, 104
De diversis, sermo 23.3
                          268, 271
De diversis, sermo 23.6   214
De diversis, sermo 40.3   252
De diversis, sermo 42.6   58
De diversis, sermo 48   8
Dominica VI post Pentecosten,
    sermo 3.4–5   263, 274
Epistola 42.6.21   261
Epistola 78.6   164
Epistola 111.1   43
Epistola 115.1   271
In ascensione Domini,
    sermo 6.7   250
In assumptione B.V.M.,
    sermo 2.5   227
In Cantica, sermo 27.iv.7   328
In Cantica, sermo 80.i.2   17
In Cantica, sermo
    85.ii.4–6   263

In nativitate Domini,
    sermo 3.4   89
In octava Paschae,
    sermo 1.7   92
In Quadragesima,
    sermo 5.1–3   274
In Quadragesima,
    sermo 5.5   180
In vigilia nativitatis Domini,
    sermo 2.6–8   164

Ps.-Bernard of Clairvaux
In Quadragesima,
    sermo 6.3   270

Boethius (Anicius Manlius
    Severinus Boethius)   123

Candidus of Fulda
Epistola, 6   123

Cassian → John Cassian

Cassiodorus
De anima, 12   113

Claudianus Mamertus
De statu animae, I.27   153–157

Gaudentius of Brescia
Sermo 13   49

Gregory the Great
In Ezechielem, I,
    hom. 8.16   197
In Ezechielem, I,
    hom. 11.5   251
In evangelia, hom. 35.1   237
Moralia in librum Job,
    XXIV.xi.32   62, 64
Moralia in librum Job,
    XXIV.xi.33   63

Regulae pastoralis, III.14   218

Ps.- Gregory the Great
   *Expositio in septem psalmos
      poenitentiales*, 19   109

Guigo I of la Chartreuse
   Meditationes, 19   134

Hildebert of Lavardin
   Epistola I.21   236
   Epistola 122.2   149
   *Vita b. Mariae
      Aegyptiacae*, I   269

Hugh of Saint-Victor
   *De institutione
      novitiorum*, 9   143
   *De sacramentis christianae
      fidei*, II.xiv.8   231
   *De sacramentis christianae
      fidei*, II.xvi.5   103
   Didascalicon, I.2   45
   Summa sententiarum,
      VI.12   131

Ps.-Hugh of Saint-Victor
   De anima, IV.11   65
   Miscellanea, I, tit. 103   116

Isidore of Seville
   Etymologiarum liber,
      XI.i.139   70
   Sententiae, II.34.4 and
      II.35   247
   Synonyma, I.77   131

Jerome (Hieronymus
   Stridonensis)
   Epistola 58.6   177

John Cassian
   Collationes, I.18   220

Ps.-Julian of Toledo
   In Nahum, 22   117
   In Nahum, 29   118, 122

Lawrence of Novara (attrib.)
   *Sermo de muliere
      Chananaea*   176

Matthew of Vendôme
   Carmina   269

Nicholas of Clairvaux
   In festo S. Andreae, sermo   29

Odo of Cluny
   Collationes, I.6   223
   Collationes, I.8   238

Ouen (Audoenus) of Rouen
   Vita s. Eligii, xv   57, 101

Peter Damian   2
   *Sermo 58 in festo
      S. Andreae*   29

Rabanus Mauris
   In Ecclesiasticum, IV.5   178

Richard of Saint-Victor
   Benjamin major, III.23   158

Seneca the Younger (L. Annaeus
   Seneca)
   *Epistulae morales ad
      Lucilium, Ep.* I.1.4   181
   *Epistulae morales ad
      Lucilium, Ep.* I.28.9   252
   *Epistulae morales ad
      Lucilium, Ep.* III.26.7   98

Index of Names and Subjects in Part One

Numbers refer to page numbers in the Introduction to the translation.

Abelard, Peter → Peter Abelard
Adam of Saint-Victor 27, 30–31
Aelred of Rievaulx 8, 15, 28
Alcher of Clairvaux 9
Ambrose of Milan 21, 38
Anne, queen of Great Britain 81
Aquinas, Thomas → Thomas
    Aquinas
Aristotle 64
Arnulf of Bohéries 4, 76
Augustine of Hippo 23, 24, 28,
    29, 35, 37–39, 41, 44, 46,
    47, 49, 59, 64, 66, 81

Baldwin of Forde 65
Batt, Antony, Benedictine
    monk 72, 75–77
  His life 75–76
  His translation of the
    Meditationes 76–77
Baudouin de Condé 61
Benedict, Rule of Saint 11–12
Bernard of Clairvaux Chapter 1
    passim, 11, 28, 35, 50–51,

53–54, 62–63, 66, 68, 72,
    76, 78–80, 84
  English translations of 4
  His renown in Europe 8
  Number of *ps.*-Bernardine
      writings 6–7, 19
  Popularity of *ps.*-Bernardine
      writings 1–8, 71
  Works attributed to
      Bernard Chapter 1
      passim
Bernard of Cluny 44
Bernard of Morlaix 12
Bernard Silvestris 71
Bernardino of Siena 24
Bonaventure, Saint 24, 33
Bullock, John 73
Bultot, Robert 19–21, 25, 26,
    28, 30–31, 44, 83–84

Cavallera, Ferdinand 6–7, 8
Chapter of Faults 11, 23, 25,
    32, 60
Compunction 58, 59, 69

Confession   28, 35, 60, 62,
    74–75, 77, 79
  Its vital importance   50–52
  Manuals for
      confessors   51–52
  Need for complete and honest
      confession   10, 16, 23, 52
Conscience/*conscientia*   8–9, 23
  And self-knowledge   9
Contemplation/*contemplatio*   10
  Defined   5–6
Courcelle, Pierre   22
Coustant, Pierre   24
Crouch, David   8
Cyril of Alexandria   38

Death in the Middle
    Ages   60–62
  Meditation on death   61–62
DelCogliano, Mark   4–5, 7
Dietz, Dom Elias   3–4, 7, 8, 10,
    16, 83

Eucharist
  Manner of receiving
      communion   14–15
  The mystery of the Eucharist
      explained   12–16

Fall of humankind, the   12,
    23–24, 37, 45–47
Freeman, R. Austin   9–10

Geoffrey of Auxerre   76
Gilson, Étienne   43
Giraud, Cédric   3, 7, 8, 20–21,
    33, 34, 83–84
Gregory the Great   29, 66,
    78–79

Grimley, Horace   82
Guigo I of la Chartreuse   27,
    29, 33
Guigo II of la Chartreuse   25, 76

Hell, descriptions of   15, 17,
    52–53, 60, 70
Henrietta Maria, Queen of
    England   76
Hildebert of Lavardin   29
Hugh of Saint-Victor   8, 24, 27,
    29, 31, 33, 35, 59, 74, 77

Ignatius of Loyola   59
Image of God   9, 13, 21–24, 37,
    40–44, 47, 70
Innocent III, Pope   16, 24,
    47–48, 50
Intellectus and
    intelligentia   41–42
Isidore of Seville   29

Janauschek, Leopold   6, 7
Javelet, Robert   21–22
Jerome   38, 66

Lateran Council, Fourth
    (1215)   51–52
Lawrence of Novara   31–32,
    66, 67
Lawson, Sister Penelope   17
Leclercq, Jean   25, 33, 71, 84
Le Goff, Jacques   53–54
Life expectancy in the twelfth
    century   16, 60
Likeness to God
  Its loss and restoration   9, 13,
      21, 22, 24, 35, 37, 40, 44,
      47–48, 65

See also Image of God, and
    Unlikeness, region of/
    regio dissimilitudinis
Love
    Its nature and importance   23,
        64–66
    Latin terms for love (*amor,
        dilectio, caritas*)   38–39
    Love and the Holy Spirit   38–
        39, 43
    Love and will   39–40

Mary, the Virgin   28
Mass → Eucharist
McManners, John   49
Meditation/*meditatio*   11, 20
    Defined   5
Meditationes piisimae
    English translations   Chapter
        5 *passim*
    Its authorship   24–25, 32–33
    Its date   33–35
    Its popularity   35, 69–70
    Its sources   26–33
        Alphabetical list of
            sources   27–28
        For details, see the *Index to
            Classical, Patristic, and
            Medieval Sources*
    Its teaching   22–23, Chapters
        3–4 *passim*
    Number of manuscripts   19–
        20, 35
    Titles given to the work   21
Memory/*memoria*   9, 42–43
Mysticism   12, 16, 28
    Distinguished from
        spirituality   5–6, 35,
        55–57

Nicholas of Gorran   24, 33
Novices, instruction of   10–12

Ouen (Audoenus) of
    Rouen   29–30

Paul VI, Pope   75
Payne, Bernard, Reverend
    Mother   68
Peifer, Claude   58, 69
Pelagius   46, 55
Penance and repentance   50,
    62–63, 79
Peter Abelard   50
Peter of Celle   7, 9
Peter Comestor   24–25, 35
Plato   64
Plotinus   64
Pons de Polignac   34
Prayer   11, 22, 31, 35, 59,
    62–63
    How to pray   66–67
    In the Rule of Saint
        Benedict   68–69
    Its nature and
        importance   66–69
    Praying and listening   67
Proclus   64
Purgatory   15, 49, 52–54
Purity of heart   10–11, 68

Raciti, Gaetano   24–25
Rancé, Armand-Jean de   61–62,
    67
Repentance → Penance and
    repentance
Richard of Saint-Victor   6, 8,
    27, 31, 33

Rochais, Henri M.   84

Self-examination   22, 35, 59
Seneca the Younger   32, 66
Sin, its nature and perils   48–50
    Mortal and venial sin   49–50
    See also Confession, and
        Penance and repentance
Solitude, need for   10
Soul, Latin terms for
    (*anima*, *animus*, *mens*,
    spiritus)   40–41
Spirituality, distinguished from
    mysticism   5–6, 35, 55–57
Stanhope, George, dean of
    Canterbury   80–82
    His life   80–81
    His translation of the
        Meditationes   81–82
Swanson, Robert   55–56

Talbot, C. Hugh   28, 84
Tanner, Norman   56–57
Taylor, Henry Osborn   26
Tears, gift of   58–59, 68–69

Teresa of Àvila   12
Thomas Aquinas   49, 50
Thomas of Froidmont   71
Thomas of Perseigne   34–35, 56
Transubstantiation   14
Trinity, doctrine of the   37–38
    Trinitarian analogies   41–42

Unlikeness, region of/*regio
    dissimilitudinis*   44

Vauchez, André   6

Wainwright, Geoffrey   55, 68
Walker, Adrian   82
Walker, Daniel   17
Warren, R., Church of England
    minister: his translation of
    the *Meditationes*   77–80
Webb, Geoffrey   82
William of Auvergne   24, 33
William of Saint-Thierry   8, 28,
    40, 43, 65, 70, 76
Worde, Wynkyn de   72–73,
    74–75